In Praise of *Los Cedros: A Tejana Memoir*

These lovingly told stories of life in the reimagined pueblo of "Los Cedros" weave an intricate tapestry of memorable characters who are familiar to any border dweller: a priest, a curandera, family members, and a young woman who says "yes" to an education and is forever changed. More than mere nostalgia, this depiction of a life that is no more due to the ever-growing militarization of the border reveals that Dorotea Reyna is a formidable wordsmith with a timely message to share.

Norma Elia Cantú
Murchison Distinguished Professor of the Humanities
Trinity University

Dorotea Reyna's excellent book, *Los Cedros: A Tejana Memoir*, takes us back to the 1960s to a small border town on the banks of the Rio Grande. Incorporating elements of fiction, this unique memoir renders vivid descriptions of a series of memorable Mexican-American residents including a priest who joins the local farm workers' quest for justice, a poet whose works are known far beyond the region, and a young girl just beginning to navigate a larger world beyond the confines of her extended family. Ultimately, Reyna's book is a compelling story about the village of "Los Cedros," both its past and its complicated present, amid rampant border militarization. Insightful and inspiring, *Los Cedros: A Tejana Memoir* will appeal to readers of all ages.

Velma García
Professor of Government
Smith College

An inspiring addition to Texas-Mexican borderlands literature. Dorotea Reyna's "little vines" (or interconnected vignettes) wonderfully make "Los Cedros" grow new green sprouts through memory and pride. May her vines forcefully climb and conquer the physical and metaphysical walls of hatred and prejudice that presently encroach the U.S.-Mexico border.

Manuel M. Martín-Rodríguez
Professor of Literature and Language
University of California-Merced

In a beautifully poetic and gently provocative memoir, Dorotea Reyna invites readers of all ages to experience the world of her childhood pueblito through loving portraits of several of its residents. Reyna juxtaposes the most tender images of her family's past with the untenable harshness of the border in the present. In so doing, she gives the reader the space to contemplate our own unique identities while feeling a part of a greater changing world, one in which we must assume our responsibility for the well-being of all.

Hilary Landorf
Assistant Vice President, Global Learning Initiatives Associate
Professor, International & Intercultural Education
Florida International University

Dorotea Reyna's *Los Cedros: A Tejana Memoir* is warm, raw, and real—it's a love letter to the author's pueblo and those who created the structure and magic within it. The vignettes that comprise *Los Cedros* are like beautiful secrets that show the reader what love looks like. This memoir is also an extraordinary example of character building within a historical context and would be an excellent model in a high school or college-level creative writing course. Reyna's accompanying Study Guide will help younger students to historically situate the text as well as to reflect on how the issues raised in *Los Cedros* personally affect them and their worldview.

Jody A. Marín
Associate Professor of English
Coordinator of Freshman and Sophomore English
Department of Language and Literature
Texas A&M University-Kingsville

Los Cedros: *A Tejana Memoir*

By Dorotea Reyna

With Study Guide

FLOWERSONG
PRESS

NOTICE: SCHOOLS AND BUSINESSES
FlowerSong Press offers copies of this book at quantity discount with bulk purchase
for educational, business, or sales promotional use. For information, please email
the Publisher at info@flowersongpress.com.
Edward Vidaurre
Publisher/Editor-in-chief
FlowerSong Press
www.flowersongpress.com

For my family

Author's Preface

Until the age of 12, I lived in a small village located on the U.S.-Mexico border in the Rio Grande Valley of South Texas. Situated on the Rio Grande River itself, my pueblo measures only .6 square miles, and as of the 2010 Census, had a population of a little more than 300 residents, three-quarters of whom lived under the federal poverty line. These are the external facts of my beloved pueblo, but they do not begin to describe the magnetic pull of this little stamp of earth on those who, like members of my family, ever had the privilege to call it home.

All but the youngest of my six siblings grew up in my village, and those of us who did speak of our pueblito in the same tones of loving reverence. Now in our later years, and as different as we are in temperaments and life journeys, we still enjoy recounting tales of our crisscrossing childhoods in that magical place. It used to worry me a bit—this passion we all felt for our pueblo—almost as if we were under a hidden spell. Perhaps it is simply childhood that holds us in its sway: that season where the imagination makes up for huge gaps in understanding, and all adults seem larger than life. Yet there was something about our pueblo that we found specifically enchanting, whether it was the beauty of fiery sunsets, or the smell of rain on our unpaved streets, or the freedom we had to roam safely all day in the woods or in our minds.

I wrote this memoir for several reasons, chief amongst them my desire to honor the people who shaped me as a child and made me who I am through their love and guidance. My memoir is a love letter to these strong influences, all dearly departed. Additionally, I want to share the profound gift of a rural childhood with my young readers, and to encourage them to embrace their lives no matter how humble their circumstances.

I also intend for my memoir to act as my own flaming sword of protection against the new deadly forces that threaten my childhood Eden, forces which include a proliferating and radicalized law enforcement presence, the deployment of powerful tools of surveillance, the expansion of the Wall, and the crimes against humanity unleashed on asylum seekers. These deadly forces also include the heightened racism across the United States perpetrated against those of a Mexican or more broadly Latino heritage. I want to push back against the false and limiting stereotypes of my people, and to reveal the true moral character of those who live in little pueblos like mine strung like gems along the border.

The memoir I have composed is of a very particular nature as it combines both facts and fiction. In a sense, all memoirs are tinged with fantasy given the very magical lens of memory. The portraits of my nuclear family, for instance, represent my *interpretation* of the facts of our shared history. The portraits of those characters outside of my immediate family, however, are definitely hybrids of fact and fancy and should ultimately be read as fiction. Father Ávila in Chapter 1, for example, is based on a real priest from my pueblo who was also a farm worker advocate and who also got into trouble for his political activism, just not in the ways I recount. I trust that the reader will grant me this poetic license as I have endeavored to stay true to the spirit of the people I write about while protecting their privacy. Likewise, I have withheld the name of my actual pueblo and rechristened it "Los Cedros" which exists nowhere on the map and yet is everywhere reflected in villages along the border.

Structurally, my chapters are written as interconnected vignettes or "little vines," weaving together snapshots-in-time of people and events. I chose this structure in lieu of a more linear, autobiographical narration to better convey the vividness of my experience. In all, I want my memoir to serve as a glimpse behind the curtain of a very particular place and time—my pueblito on the border in the 60s.

Part of the lure for me to write this work is that mysterious sense I have of remaining in conversation with my village. There is something tangibly alive about my relationship with my pueblo that transcends space and time, as real as a blood vessel connecting our very flesh.

Dorotea Reyna
Pacifica, California

Contents

"Let us make human beings in our image, according to our likeness."

--Genesis 1:26

Chapter 1: Father Ávila
Activist priest

The first thing you noticed about Father Ávila were his eyebrows jutting out like the burning bush on the mountain. His eyes were a deep, pure brown, and when he smiled, you noticed that they were golden with small black flecks like pebbles under a rushing river. His face, however, was not often caught smiling. No, it was often furrowed in a concentrated focus, much like the eagle when it has spied its prey.

It was a gaze of utter penetration, separating the sins of man from the luminous divine, or, in more earthly terms, truth from hypocrisy. At 46, his ruddy face was handsome to look at, if one were ever tempted to see Father Ávila in that mundane, sensual way. His large curved nose was of particular note, and with his piercing gaze and prominent eyebrows gave that sense again of an eagle ready to pounce. His firm chin, now lined with the sorrows of the world, was graced with a single cleft. His mouth was firm and almost always set in a straight line like a judge at the moment of verdict.

At 5'8", Father Ávila stood tall above many in his congregation and his shoulders were broad as if he lifted weights. They had the energy of a man of action and seemed to be always moving, pulling him forward. As the years had gone by, his torso had grown broader, although he was not the type of man to step on a scale to see if he indeed weighed 168 pounds. There was no time for that.

Altogether he gave the appearance of leonine strength and an unquestioned ferocity of purpose. His cassock swirled as he walked and was often the only thing seeming to move in the sweltering heat. He was not the kind of priest the children were later to meet: the jovial young priests in their first assignments, the ones upon whom they would gleefully throw themselves, grabbing their hands and twirling like on a merry-go-round. You wanted to embrace Father Ávila, but he was the kind of priest who engendered awe and perhaps a little fear. He was the judgment side of God's face.

Father Ávila had been in Los Cedros for a little over a year now, and this rural assignment, so different from his years in San Antonio, suited his quiet soul. At times he missed the grandeur of the big church covered in gold and bedecked with flowers, with thousands of people in the congregation for which he served as assistant pastor, and the daily Masses, and the three large Masses on Sunday. He missed the city's old families celebrating weddings, baptisms and quinceañeras, and the festivity of the meals to which he was invited. Here he was more often treated to a dinner of jackrabbit, killed the day before and tasting of gunpowder, a cantaloupe or watermelon, or a basket of pan dulce.

His problems in San Antonio began when he started beseeching the Bishop to pay heed to what he was hearing on the news and watching before his very eyes. There was a spirit of unrest amongst the poor Mexican workers in this bustling city, and rumors of a man named César Chávez who believed that the poor should organize to address their suffering. Father Ávila had seen him on TV explaining his rationale for the strikes he was organizing in the lush vineyards of California, and felt that the Church had a role to play in La Causa. The Bishop did not see things his way, especially when he heard through the clerical grapevine that Father Ávila was expounding these opinions during Sunday Mass.

In Los Cedros, Father Ávila found himself assigned to the polar opposite of his congregation in San Antonio, outlawed to this tiny pueblito that dotted the Rio Grande River. This exile would be the pattern for the rest of his days, assigned optimistically to one parish before he was unceremoniously bounced to another, less visible, one. These transfers would sometimes happen within a few years, even with the priest shortage which was already beginning to be felt.

These decisions were never easy for the Bishop because Father Ávila was, in every other way, an excellent priest. Highly intelligent, he had studied in Italy for over a year and was a gifted scholar and interpreter of the Bible. He was also a powerful orator and had the gift of holding spellbound an entire congregation, whether they be dozens or hundreds in number. Most of all, he was deeply a man of God and had never experienced the crises of faith suffered by other men and women of the cloth. There was no shadow of doubt between him and

2

his calling. He was as faithful as a sundial, as steadfast as God's love for all of humankind.

He had an attractive air about him, a charisma, that drew people of all stations of life to his company. He could converse as easily with affluent Anglo parishioners as with the humblest Mexicano slipping into the back of the church. His confidence in God and in his priestly mission radiated throughout his person and he was never alone for any of the holidays, especially Christmas and Easter. Whether at a large church or small, his dance card, as they say, was always full.

It stung him to be transferred to what his fellow priests considered at the time to be the rural hinterlands—the frontera—not for the sake of wounded pride, though there was some of that, but more for the loss of scope. Father Ávila was a talented man, and talent well knows its power, if not its perimeter. He felt he had done an excellent job organizing this busy urban church, and yet, there was so much more to do in building up the parish school.

There was even more troubling to him the pang of being disappointed in the Bishop and some of the more conservative members in his brotherhood of priests. He felt again the pain of childhood when his grandmother stopped him from playing marbles with a poor, dirty child in his barrio—that sense of amazement that someone you loved and looked up to had such a different sense of right and wrong. At 46, he had known his share of disappointments in others, but the lack of faith in him shown by the Bishop particularly smote his heart. Maybe it was because of the many rich conversations he had enjoyed with the Bishop at the latter's comfortable sacristy, generally over a glass of Spanish sherry brought to them by the kindhearted woman who served the Bishop as his housekeeper.

At first, it felt like a meteor crashing into a planet, this coming to a pueblito with 100 families and 300 citizens in total. Nor was this his only congregation; the Diocese had given him responsibility for three small pueblos—the furthest 16 miles away—and so his busy week was spent driving to each tiny church, offering Mass at least once during the weekdays, and then Saturday confessions at one of the parishes and Sunday Mass at all three of his congregations.

Soon, however, his capacity found its purpose as an artist settles upon the canvas once he takes the first few brush strokes. The days fell into a regular pattern and he was grateful for the help of Margarita and women like her who washed his vestments and the altar cloths, making them every bit as immaculate as when he was stationed in San Antonio, where occasionally his special vestments were sent out for dry cleaning. He loved the humble people he served and found pleasure in the friendship and patronage of the few educated parishioners, all teachers. In Los Cedros, Mass was offered at 6:00 AM and he enjoyed the quiet of that hour with the sun staining the sky a rosy pink. He grew accustomed to the piercing cries of the roosters before this hour—every home had its flock of chickens—and the faint sounds of dogs, cows and pigs blended in with the bells of the Angelus.

On Saturdays, he heard confessions and there he learned the secret recesses of his parishioners' hearts: from the seven-year-old boy grudgingly relating the story of punching his sister, to the teen girl tearfully confessing her pregnancy, to the wife angry at her husband for spending too much time at the cantina, and the husband thinking of a woman not his own. He knew with the acumen of a skilled psychologist that the sins they shared were only a fraction of the real danger to their souls, yet he was patient and accepted their take of things, letting the truth expand and reveal itself over time. Notwithstanding his patience, his flock trembled at the sound of his deep voice giving them their penance. Nor God, nor Father Ávila, were to be taken lightly.

Not that Father Ávila was without his vanities. He enjoyed listening to Italian opera broadcast from Mexico City after the last Mass was said on Sunday afternoon. He enjoyed good food and good wine, and loved to talk about great meals of which he had partaken. Once, when he was invited to breakfast at one of his parishioner's homes and was served a stack of pancakes, he took one and wrapped it around his chorizo and eggs, calling it a "crepe." The year he had spent in Rome on scholarship, he had fully enjoyed Italy's cuisine and great art, and also relished with fond memories his travels through Spain and France.

He considered himself an educated, cultured man, but his little vanities were never intended to make someone feel lesser than. He loved the paintings of the Italian Renaissance, but had to make do with a dark and rather extreme rendition of St. Michael slaying the demon in a painting floating above the parishioners' heads as they blessed themselves with Holy Water exiting Mass. He loved stained glass windows and was glad that the little churches he served all had them, simple as the designs might be.

He insisted that his vestments be spotlessly clean and that the women who prepared them know which color of chasuble was appropriate for the season. He did not enjoy babies fussing and crying throughout services and was not reluctant to ask mothers to take them outside. He wanted every one of his oratories to be heard by the flock, especially by the sinners who most needed to hear them. He insisted on women wearing veils, and little girls, at the very least, Kleenex tissue doilies pinned down with bobby pins. Although he insisted on no other dress code, it still pleased him on Easter to see men observing the Holy Day by sporting dark suits and starched white collars, and the women blooming in lovely pastel dresses—blue, lilac, yellow, pink, green—like spring wildflowers. Most of all, he never hesitated to express his opinions, even with the Bishop and other more timid peers. He was sure of his mind and sure of his God.

The only restraint he had for exercising a bit more luxury, say going to the movies or eating out, was the paltry monthly stipend the Church afforded him. Even decades later, he continued to thank the parishioners who had once a month slipped an extra $10 into his hands. He was too proud to say that such generosity had been vital, for in truth, Father Ávila had occasionally gone hungry when such manna did not rain from the heavens.

Before his transfer to the frontera, he remembered his last conversation with the Bishop. Once again, they were discussing the Indian-featured Mexicano that had appeared seemingly out of nowhere and overnight to publicize the plight of farm workers in California. When that thundercloud had yet to reach Texas, the Bishop, like Father Ávila, was more inclined to spontaneously support La Causa. It was only when Mr. Chávez traveled to Texas to do the same for the workers in the fields picking endless miles of citrus, sugar cane, melons, onions, and potatoes that their conversations took a turn. While a predominantly Mexican-American parish, the grand Catholic Church Father Ávila served also counted a fair number of Anglo growers who were not at all comfortable with talk of Chávez organizing their workers.

The Bishop, aware that more than half of the Diocese's support came from this eternally vigilant sector, tried to caution Father Ávila that his sermons on the plight of the farm workers were falling on rocky soil towards the front of the church.

"Our Lord is the Savior of both growers and farm workers, Rene."

To which Father Ávila replied, "Yes, Bishop, but the Lord never intended for one group in His Kingdom to enslave another. We were all created equally in His image."

Often, after Saturday afternoon confessions in San Antonio, Father Ávila would reflect upon the sins that he had not heard confessed:

"Bless me, Father, for I have sinned. I only pay my workers 70 cents an hour for picking cantaloupe ten hours a day, seven days a week, during the three months of harvest."

"Bless me, Father, for I have sinned. I provide my workers with no bathrooms, no medical facilities and no clean drinking water. Instead, they are forced to drink from dirty puddles."

"Bless me, Father, for I have sinned. It matters little to me that children are stooping in the hot sun, picking crops with their parents, and that their itinerant lives make it necessary for them to stay out of school for a third of the year."

No, these were sins he never heard confessed nor ever expected to hear confessed.

***

The news of the planned strike had electrified the Valley for almost six months. The pan-state farm workers' strike centered on César Chávez leading a march from Rio Grande City to the State Capitol at Austin, a journey which would take two months in total. At issue were worker demands for contracts and hourly salaries of $1.25, water breaks, and access to bathrooms. Chávez had beseeched the Catholic Bishops for their support, but it would be months before a committee of bishops voted to wholeheartedly give their endorsement.

As the date for the strike neared, there were rumors that the Governor would call on the Border Patrol to stop any attempts to block commerce along the border, including on bridges between the U.S. and Mexico. Already, a fearsome specter gathered along the frontera, their numbers prepared to swell and become even more intimidating.

Unbeknownst to many of his fellow priests, much less the Bishop, Father Ávila had agreed to join the strike for the first leg of the march from Rio Grande City to Raymondville, a distance of 75 miles. He had enlisted the support of a sympathetic visiting priest from Monterrey who would take over his duties during the week that he planned to be away, and accepted a ride from a parishioner who was participating in the march after the close of his first Sunday Mass at 8:00 am.

As the front-page news story in the McAllen Monitor later documented, Father Ávila would walk beside César Chávez and the leaders of the march flanked by UFW flags and behind the brilliant tapestry of the Virgin of Guadalupe. The choice of the chasuble to commemorate this momentous occasion had been known only to him. He chose the color that was appropriate for the Holy Days of Easter, including Palm Sunday and Good Friday. He chose the red.

Chapter 2: Margarita
Caregiver

When you hugged her, the first thing you noticed was her smell; if lovingkindness had a scent, this would be it. The next thing you noticed was the coolness of her skin, the delicious mounds of her feminine sweetness. Her name was Margarita, and she was as unassuming as those delicate and fragrant flowers growing in every garden: the flor de lantana with its tiny parasols of yellow and pink, and its sticky leaves rough as a kitten's tongue.

She was small of stature, even the girl at ten was almost her height, but heavy in torso. Her skin was fair and her eyes a soft green, and she kept her ill-cut hair short and held back off her face with bobby pins or cheap plastic barrettes. Her clothes were handmade and unadorned, and when she watched the children, she wore a small yellow and white gingham apron.

She was 53 years of age and lived with her invalid mother, taking care of her after the stroke. Her two younger sisters were married and had children. She was single, and so the task of caregiver fell upon her. Not that she saw caring for her mother as a task, although lately, trying to decipher the words her mother shouted at her in frustration was a challenge, as were her daily baths and schedule of medicines.

In the summers, she would watch the children of the neighbors who were teachers when the latter worked extra months. There were four children and they were a lively handful, especially the boy and middle sister, who were prone to popping off the screens of their bedroom windows and escaping naptime for forays into the plaza or the "lagoon," that section of the river framed on both banks by an abundance of trees which towered above an otherwise flat terrain. She worried, especially when they ran to play in the lagoon, because of the rumors of things not of this world haunting its depths. Her simple faith admitted the existence of evil, but she was helpless to stop the children from their mischievous, willful ways.

Although she had watched them for a few years now, they still took her authority lightly, as even children knew that there was not a truly angry bone in her body. Her voice was soft and low, and even when they exasperated or frightened her, never raised. They loved to take her by the hands and twirl her round and round, or scramble between her legs as she exclaimed, "You kids, wait until I tell your Father!" Whether in fact she reported their poor behavior to their parents was doubtful, however, as they were never subsequently chastened. Most often she was found laughing because the children could easily make her laugh, and her eyes twinkled at their impish ways when those jokes were not at her expense.

Besides caring for her mother and watching the children, her other major focus was washing the vestments and altar cloths for Father Ávila. It was the day of soaking the heavy whites in hot water and bleach, then putting them through a wringer to extract the moisture. Every week there were vestments to wash and hang, and altar cloths to carefully press and avoid singeing the delicate lace before laying them out on the altar before Mass. It was also the days when, other than preparing the altar for Mass, as a woman she was never allowed to otherwise step on this sacred site. Margarita was also responsible for sweeping and mopping the church floors using the pine-scented oil that constituted clean to every nose, as well as for dusting the pews, sometimes with her young charges tagging along. She also polished the chalice and the plates for communion, giving these holy vessels a luminous shine.

She performed her tasks with a quiet, capable cheerfulness, and no one had ever heard her utter the words "No" or "I can't" or "Why" much less the words "I need" or "I want." Resentment was not part of her makeup.

As the only unmarried woman in her matriarchal family, she was also expected to help sew children's dresses for special occasions using patterns she bought from the store in the larger town twenty miles away. Her fortunate nieces boasted red velveteen dresses with pearl buttons and white scalloped collars for Christmas, and violet taffeta dresses with lace trim for Easter. Her two sisters also sewed, but all agreed that her hand was the best, and occasionally, she even sewed for them.

And so it was on a bright Saturday afternoon that she found herself in the midst of a birthday party for her niece who had just turned 12. Not only had she sewn her dress, but her younger sister's dress as well, and they were visions of loveliness in their matching white outfits with eyelet sleeves and blue sashes. She had also helped to prepare the meal for the family members and neighbors present, as well as the towering pink cake now lit with 12 candles after the piñata had been burst and its divine gifts conquered and divided.

It was 5:00 PM when Margarita finally sat down to take a sip of her lemonade, smiling with happiness and flushed with laughter, as children scooped up candy and the first sharp pains traveled down her arm.

Chapter 3: Doña Isabel
Curandera

The children in the neighborhood called her a witch, and that was just one reason Doña Isabel gave the girl pause. Her sun-darkened face had so many wrinkles, seemingly millions of them looped across her face, that it was hard to see her eyes or indeed any of her features. She lived in a one room house by the church and across the weed-stubbled baseball field. Outside her door, she kept a large barrel which collected rain for drinking water. Once the girl had looked into it and it seemed unfathomably deep with shadowy reflections of the bright blue Texas sky. The water was sweet then, and she would offer you a ladle pulled from its dark, clean depths.

Maybe too it was the manner in which she moved, so slowly that time seemed to have stood still, but somehow floating slightly above the ground because her footsteps did not drag. She would catch you by surprise like that, appearing out of nowhere around the corners of her home. Her yard was packed dirt, littered with pebbles and broken glass, and her home was scarcely separate from the two other small houses close by; collectively, they inscribed a triangle.

Did she ever hear Doña Isabel speak? The girl must have, but couldn't remember the sound of her voice. Perhaps because she was so old or perhaps for other reasons, she kept her speech and her ways to herself.

The girl had been inside her home only a few times when her mother visited Doña Isabel and brought her a plate of food or inquired about her health. Because there was only one chair, the girl would sit on the hard bed by the wood plank shelves supporting a flock of votive candles: Nuestra Señora de San Juan, San Martín de Porres, Sagrado Corazón de Jesús, and one other votive candle that always seemed to the girl to be out of place because nowhere in the church had she ever seen it repeated. Later she learned that the image on the candle, the same votive her Abuela had, was that of Don Pedro Jaramillo, Master Healer, curandero. Although she never saw this candle in the churches, she saw it often in the homes of this and other pueblitos. Don Pedrito was revered and considered a Saint.

There was one time she came over to Doña Isabel's home which was so confusing and disconcerting that she never forgot it. Her mother would from time to time take hot meals to Doña Isabel, especially on special days like Christmas or Easter, but on this day, the foil-covered plate was given to the girl as her own task. She walked up to the open door to Doña Isabel's home, and because it was too dark to see inside, she entered with her whole nine-year-old body. What she saw was Doña Isabel praying over a woman lying in her bed, sweeping her body with a bundle of herbs, as she recited the Our Father in Spanish: "Padre Nuestro que estás en los cielos." In that bewildering moment, the girl saw the clear bowl of water under the bed within which floated an egg yolk.

She did not remember where she laid the plate of food or what she told her mother when she came home. The scene was beyond comprehension to her; she had no words to describe it. To this day, she had never shared this memory with her brothers and sisters. It was almost as if she had momentarily entered a portal into another universe and thought it better to keep this mysterious experience to herself.

Father Ávila, of course, was well aware of Doña Isabel's vocation as a healer. In a pueblo of 300 residents, there was not a lot he did not know about his flock. And part of his flock Doña Isabel most certainly was; she was amongst a handful of women who attended 6:00 AM daily Mass and he appreciated her fidelity, even though as a modern priest, he was dubious and fairly judgmental about her profession. His own eyes told him, however, that this vocation came to Doña Isabel as a calling and not as a way to take money from others.

She was not only one of the most faithful in his small congregation, but also one of the poorest in a place where most people were from exceedingly humble circumstances. The small coins she pressed into the collection basket from time to time represented well the teaching of the widow's mite. For her part and at her age, she never considered for a moment that she was different from any other parishioner, but perhaps there was some talk.

Truth be told, they were both healers of the soul. Unlike those that came to confession, the desperate people who came to her door rarely needed to return. She had helped many pregnant women, a quiet little girl who never smiled, and a man who was losing his sight. She also protected people from the evil eye as well as sustos caused by various traumas. She never asked for payment, but was sometimes given a wrinkled dollar bill, or a basket of oranges, or a small bloody sack of white-winged doves.

She took up so little space in this pueblo of small houses and poor people, and spoke so few words, that her life was almost invisible. And so Father Ávila quietly blessed the small jars of water she would from time to time bring to him after Mass.

Chapter 4: Girl
My story

If you had asked the girl directly when she was at the tender age of eight or nine to describe Los Cedros, she would have answered "Yes!" to your request with great excitement. In her imagination, she would take you by the hand and walk you around her enchanted kingdom, which is how she perceived her pueblo. She would eagerly tell you how the paved highway through mesquite-dotted terrain would end, suddenly, on an unpaved road going in two directions: straight before you and to your right. At this very entrance to her world, and to the left, she would point out an unusually tall brake of lush green trees, crowded and dense, to which she had never been and was in fact prohibited to explore, that fertile crescent which the children called the lagoon.

But it was to the right where her stories would begin, at that turn off the highway to those gray stones blazing hot from the sun and shining always with iridescent hints of blue and violet. She would tell you about the baseball field to the left and the post office to the right, and point out the small, yellow church like a butterfly at rest. With growing enthusiasm, she would describe the cluster of houses which circumscribed her world: her own house, where she lived with her parents and younger siblings, and across the street her grandparents' home, belonging to her Abuelo and Abuela, where she spent most of her time in childhood.

She was most excited about the huge cedar tree separating her home from the street, a tree so large it seemed like another grandfather to her with its wavy, scaly back and its many branches and leaves like salty needles. This was indeed her magic perch as she spent countless hours leaning back against its trunk and lost in rapture as she gazed up at the cloud kingdoms blooming in the deep blue sky.

Down the street from her Abuelo's house, she could describe the camposanto to the right, which she glanced at with wonder but never visited during the day and hurried past quickly with her sister at dusk. The cemetery, gaily bedecked with colorful ribbons, plastic flowers, and sometimes pinwheels, seemed magical to her by day, but by night and guarded only by a simple wooden gate, it frightened her little soul.

Further down the street and to the left, she could tell you about the small grocery store with the blind dog known for its wicked bite who lay sleeping at its threshold. You would have to really want ice cream to brave this dog and jump over its slumbering form to enter the tiendita. On long, hot summer days, the children calculated this risk was well worth it, and one by one, they would hop over this Cerberus to enter the dark sweet interior within. She would delight in telling you about the luscious ice cream flavors you could buy there—strawberry, vanilla, and chocolate of course—plus all sorts of sherbet—with vapors of ice hanging over the containers when the grocer lifted the glass case.

She could also tell you where the ferry was next to the Border Patrol station, while across the rushing river, a luxuriant bank of trees, the same that framed the lagoon, demarcated a land called Mexico. In many ways, the bank on the far side of the river looked just like the bank on her side of the river, but perhaps greener, more tropical, with a hint of foreignness.

Yes, she could take you around the entire perimeter of Los Cedros, a distance of a few miles, without any difficulty at all though she would get lost in navigating the little tangle of interior connecting streets that made up the part of her pueblo with the most houses. From the age she could walk with her brother and sister around this oblong circumscribing her village, she could describe every general point of interest, as well as the places of specific interest and importance to her: her own home and that of her abuelos, the little church behind them, the overarching cedar tree.

The mystery remains, however, why Los Cedros would ever have chosen her to recount its stories.

For, outside the simple street plan of her pueblo, the stark geometry which anyone could describe, there was so much that escaped her. She could not, for example, remember what relation to the family were the old couple who lived beside her abuelos and who she visited from time to time. She could remember her "Tía's" toothless smile, the faint mustache over her lips, her kind twinkling eyes that embraced you as soon as she saw you, but she never understood, even after years of visits, why or how she was her 'Tía' or her husband 'Tío' with his shock of wavy white hair and startling blue eyes.

This web of connections, so vital to her parents and grandparents and so rooted in the pueblo's history, utterly escaped her. As a child, she kept this secret shame to herself, and indeed she felt guilty to not be able to connect and hence honor the many kind relatives who embraced her eagerly when they saw her, lighting upon her name as belonging to the eldest daughter of her parents.

Furthermore, unlike her brother, she did not know the many places from which she was prohibited or exiled herself: the lagoon, the cemetery, the river by the ferry, the second plaza and little store, the pool hall. These were mysteries sealed to her her entire life.

By nature and nurture, there were many vital aspects of Los Cedros that she was never going to be able to describe, not ever.

Yet, even before her parents fully understood her, Los Cedros knew why she would fulfill the mission it entrusted to her notwithstanding her many temperamental flaws. The very traits that made it so hard for her to focus on the external world in all its dazzling detail prepared her for this task: her inward turning gaze, by which she focused on what fascinated her with the keenness of a scientist; her habit of binding herself intensely to that which she loved; and the high fidelity of her listening through which nary a word of truth escaped her.

The unusual quality about this girl for a child so young was how deeply she pulled the world inside her, both through her eyes and through her ears, as well as her habit of personalizing the sights and sounds of her world, holding them close and making them inextricably hers.

The scenes of her pueblo delighted her and captured her imagination. The clouds and flowers, most particularly, seemed to her a hidden language which could be deciphered if one were patient enough, still enough, or loved them enough. Hours she spent in the cedar tree leaning back carefully against its wide curving trunk, looking up through the branches and needles to the large puffy clouds continuously reshaping by the minute. Here a castle, there a full-sailed ship, she often imagined what it would be like to actually walk inside the clouds as her own secret kingdom with pavilions of lavender and blue.

If she could rouse her active younger sister to play this game, they would each choose a blossoming cloud kingdom for her own, for some of the clouds were so large and so slow-moving that you could actually imagine living there over the span of an hour. She would also coax her sister to name her special stars as the first pinpoints of light pricked the dusk. This inclination to love natural objects and claim them as her own pursued her for most of her childhood.

So too, she was captivated by the small yet brilliant gardens in Los Cedros, the ones lighting up with dazzling colors the simple houses. Every home had its share of glory. Her Abuela's home had flowers on her front porch and in the two small gardens to each side. Off to the left side of the porch, where she and Abuelo spent many an hour, was a blazing esperanza bush with its cascades of trumpet-shaped blossoms ending in a simple scallop. She and her siblings would mirthfully pop the nascent buds on their foreheads: it seemed to them a stroke of magical good luck. In the rain, these radiant gold blossoms seemed to shiver in their frail silk robes.

To the left side of Abuela's home, the garden featured a magical wild orchid tree; "pata de vaca," cow's foot, is what the small tree was called in Spanish, but the girl's ear discarded this name completely as doing no justice to its exquisite pink and violet blossoms. This tree was harder for her to sit in for its closely interwoven branches were thinner than those of the cedar tree, but as a small child she would find a way to ensconce herself, surrounded by butterfly-shaped mirrors. These moments would enchant her, and later served her as a reference for the truth that beauty could be found anywhere, even in a humble garden with scraggly hens running to and fro.

It was the garden to the right of the house which most entranced her, for it was here that a throng of hollyhocks bloomed like totem poles into the azure Texas sky. The fact that the hollyhocks dwarfed even her grandmother astonished the girl, as well as the way they grew up the ladder of their stems from multiple blossoms at the base to the gradually singular blossoms up towards the apex, all this splendor in a full circle radius. Most of all, she was dazzled by their colors: white, yellow, rose, red, dark purple, and in her mind's eye, she clearly saw the rarest and most alluring of all the hollyhocks: the blue hollyhocks.

As an adult, it came as a shock to her that the blue hollyhocks did not exist. In her mind she returned to the garden over and again to reimagine the hollyhocks, reciting their colors under her breath as she surveyed them through the gaze of memory. How could she be so wrong about this? The blue hollyhocks were her favorite, the ones to whom she told her secrets as they always seemed to listen. It was this gap between reality and her imagination that most marked the girl, but this fatal flaw—or divine gift—was well hidden behind her serious dark eyes and black bangs for many, many years.

Not only did the girl drink in the world through her eyes, but also through her ears, acutely so, to a degree which startled her parents and other adults. Her mother was thus startled when, bathing the girl as a toddler in the kitchen sink, her daughter looked up at her with indignation and hissed, "Pero me prometiste!" Indeed, early on in her life, promises of any sort—for a bedtime story or an ice cream cone or an extra hour up to watch a beloved movie—were commitments she never let anyone forget.

Since she was a very quiet child, adults could not fathom how carefully she was listening, absorbing words and the tones in which they were expressed with rapt intensity. Sometimes it was the words themselves that arrested her, sometimes it was the tones, making her hone into an eavesdropped conversation with even greater concentration. Mysteriously, the words that entered her most deeply were the comforting words she heard in Church. These settled very deeply into the foundation of her being and were never to be dislodged through fire or storm.

She was a very well brought up child with parents that were wholly dedicated to their duty. Her father, especially, was the children's moral guide, and often he would stoop to his knees with his arms around their shoulders carefully explaining the why of things. Why it was wrong, for example, to disobey their mother or fight with one another as brothers and sisters. He himself had been adopted by his uncle after his mother died, and it was this man and his wife that the children called Abuelo and Abuela. Estranged from his siblings, who remained with his suddenly widowed father, he could not bear to see his own children tangled in playground combat. The children very quickly learned what was right and what was wrong, and these clearly marked and daily reinforced moral posts made their family life simple and happy.

She found it more difficult to have her mother for her own, for there were many children. Throughout the day, her mother moved like a quick phantasm in the cycle of her many tasks: getting her brood ready for school, or Church, or bed; sweeping, mopping, and washing dishes; washing loads of clothes and hanging them out to dry; and emerging out of the kitchen, seemingly out of nowhere, with concocted miracles like vanilla cake with seven-minute frosting piled in stiff, sweet waves.

It was the 60s and her parents both taught in public schools half an hour's drive away; her mother had earned a degree in science and her father one in history. Because they had struggled so mightily in college to give presentations in English back when her father said there were just enough Mexican students to form a baseball team, they sent their children to a Catholic school where the students were a mix of white and Mexican children and where their teachers, who were all white, were a mix of lay people and nuns. Her parents' choice of schooling created the first fissure in the girl's psyche—between that period of her life when she felt whole and unbroken, and the subsequent period where she would always see the world as divided into two.

Spanish was her first language, although she never remembered the time her parents described when she sang in Spanish. At some point in her very young consciousness, her parents began speaking to her almost exclusively in English, and thereafter, she was always careful to distinguish and separate the two *idiomas*. Even at the age of five, she had already divined the magical potency of language and was careful not to intertwine these two exclusive powers, these competing kingdoms, Spanish and English. Her discovery of the sorcery of language was fueled by the set of encyclopedias her parents had purchased from a traveling salesman: twelve leather-bound volumes, maroon and white with gilt letters—the first three volumes for children, the latter nine for adults including history, science and psychology. At what age she fell into the pool of fairytale and rhyme in the children's volumes, she could not remember, but when language, especially poetry, pulled her into its embrace, she was never again to let go.

Her father read to the children at night, sending them off to sleep with delightful music played on a small record player. He was a modern, educated man and knew how to sharpen and grow young minds through music and storytelling. At some point, she began reading the fairytale and poetry books on her own and spent countless hours bewitched by the colorful and fanciful illustrations of queens and castles, princes and dragons, and fair-haired shepherd boys in villages so distant from her own yet so close. She liked to recite poems under her breath, loving the lilt of the lines as they converged in meaning.

Going to school with so many white children, the sons and daughters of store owners and farmers, was like stepping into one of her fairytales. It was another world, a world which terrified her a little, with teachers who were tall and some stern. It was a time when the paddle swung freely and also the ruler, the latter used to rap open palms as a punishment for Mexican children who unconsciously slipped into Spanish. She was never punished this way, for she had learned to separate these two languages well before she entered first grade.

So began six long years of learning the secrets of the alphabet and numbers, of reading and writing essays, and of diagramming sentences. She excelled academically early on and never wavered, for along with her dreamy imagination, which she kept to herself, concentration was her constant companion, almost a genie she could summon at will. Unlike the other children who got into trouble for wiggling or getting out of their desks or not keeping their hands and feet to themselves, she was always at one with the lesson before her. Eventually, she came to prefer writing essays above all other assignments—making visible the dreamy habits of her imagination as she compared and contrasted the pinks of the dawn with the rosy orange of the skies at sunset—yet she was equally faithful to her arithmetic lesson, carefully lining up the numbers in multiplication or division, waiting for the right answer which clicked in her ear like a little clasp.

She had far more freedom of being and expression at her Abuelo's home where the children stayed after school and on weekends, as well as on the long, hot days of summer when they would idly watch cartoons by splaying themselves on the plastic couch and sucking on popsicles. What joy to eat snow cones made by her Abuelo from shaved ice with syrup; their tongues were often an exaggerated purple, red and blue. They also delighted in the daily stack of tortillas her Abuela made—one stack of flour tortillas, the other of corn—which they drenched in butter.

Her Abuela was a small woman with the plump arms and hips of women in her village. Even from the beginning, she always seemed old, her silver hair braided in a thin crown that she wore across her head and fastened down with rhinestone combs. Her dresses were always handmade, with small buttons and the breast pockets edged with simple lace.

Even though her grandmother was rarely jovial and given to restrained bursts of anger at the passersby who roared past her porch in their cars or pickups without stopping to visit, the girl loved her ardently. She shadowed her Abuela in her daily round of chores: now the kitchen where she cooked at the stove and washed dishes in a basin, now the garden where she searched for errant hens before they were put away in large cages for the night.

What the girl most remembered was the savory dishes that would come from her Abuela's hands, especially the guisado with the tender steak she cut into small pieces and stewed in a broth of onions, bell pepper and comino, or the calabacitas with its beguiling mixture of zucchini and corn. They lived in an agricultural area, so the tomatoes were always fresh, as were the watermelon and cantaloupe their grandfather cut with a mighty rusted knife. Milk was delivered door to door, and the girl did not remember eating much canned food beyond the occasional canned meat sold at the small combination grocery store and butcher shop a few blocks away.

Her Abuela lived to her 80s, one breast withered from cancer, and one eye blue from glaucoma. Even in her presence, her grandmother seemed magically absent as if she were a time traveler from another century. Vivid in the girl's memory were singular scenes centered on her Abuela: standing under a naked light bulb below a bright moon as she skinned a rabbit Abuelo had just killed—the same rabbit which would then appear on the table deliciously seasoned with gunshot—or alone in her garden at dusk surrounded by the hollyhocks which encased her and towered above her head.

Her grandfather was a different cipher altogether, and a force with which to be reckoned. Whereas her grandmother was submissive, complaining only under her breath, Abuelo was a domineering lion who ruled over all their lives, including his son's, their father. Large and heavy set, he dressed every day in khakis and wore a straw sombrero permanently stained with sweat. He also wore heavy black shoes which he ordered the girl to remove when he was tired, laying them on her knee. He often ordered her to fetch him a ladle of water, his instructions always the same: half the ladle was to come from the rain barrel by the door, half from the pitcher Abuela had already made cold in the refrigerator. A child of exact nature, the girl always did as she was told, although it frightened her to open the refrigerator from time to time and see a bloody goat's head.

He was a man of many lives and had worked in the Houston shipyards, and later driven a bus taking the señoras from small villages along the highway to shop in the larger town half an hour away where her parents taught and the children went to school. He also taxied shoppers from "el otro lado" who came by ferry to shop in that same town; his blue Falcon was always in use.

Abuelo could be jovial and abrupt and shouted to his wife to attend to him all through the day and night. As the children's Spanish gradually began to fade, he would threaten in frustration that he was going to send them to Monterrey to learn their proper native tongue. How often the girl had heard to her shame: "¡Les voy a mandar a

Monterrey!" The oft-repeated threat also planted in her brain the notion that there was another Mexico from the one she could glimpse beyond the river—one with large cities and sophisticated schools where her native language flowed freely and was cherished as the lifeblood of a proud culture.

Because they were old, her grandparents only went to Mass from time to time and so Father Ávila would occasionally bring them Communion on their front porch. It always seemed to the girl a strange clash of worlds, that of her grandfather who unapologetically shouted and cursed all day long, and that of the stern but patient priest who gave them the Host with a serious, penetrating face. Those were the only times that her Abuelo seemed for the span of fifteen minutes, meek.

The girl also passionately loved her grandfather, and because she was the oldest child with an alert and questioning mind, he would pay her special attention. One way he would show his bias was in gifting her with quarters while at the same time her younger brother and sister received only dimes and nickels. She would return the quarter to him and righteously refuse it because it was unfair to her siblings, demanding that he divide the money equally, at which he would roar with laughter because he found her virtue not admirable, but humorous. She used to think him very rich as he jiggled all the loose change in his deep pockets. It was only later she discovered that real money was very quiet.

And so she spent her years shuttling between home and school, the place where she always had to be vigilant among strangers, and the place where she could more easily be herself. Both worlds had ironclad rules. She remembered the time her sister and brother sauntered down the street back home after escaping naptime through the easy latches on the windows; this time, they were met by Abuelo standing in the middle of the road and waiting for them with his heavy belt in his hand. She remembered running to him and begging him not to spank them, but his face was resolute and she doesn't remember what happened after that.

Because of her inquisitive mind, she often got away with things that might be considered impertinent, the time, for example, she questioned Father Ávila about a seeming paradox in one of the Bible tales he told at Mass. He was eating breakfast with her family and she remembers the way he glanced down at her with quick irritation before looking over disapprovingly at her parents. Later, she dared not question any of her teachers; the only adult she could ply with questions on the why of things, mostly on issues of right and wrong, was her father. She was silent about her disagreements with authority all throughout her childhood; at puberty, the dam of restraint came crashing down and she became, as if overnight, openly defiant.

If there were things the girl was charmed by, there were other things she simply turned her mental gaze away from—that is, the harsher aspects of life. She lived in the country, and so her neighbors across the street had a pigpen with fierce smells and to her eyes, horrifying activity. So too the little grocery store where she bought her ice cream cones was also a butcher shop with the heavy smell of freshly-killed carcasses hanging in the air. She tried not to let her gaze go beyond the counter where the grocer took her coins, but inevitably, she would spy a carcass surrounded by flies that slowly buzzed around it. Nor could she stop her ears from the anguished cries of the cows as they were being slaughtered.

That part of Los Cedros, the struggle of nature at its rawest, was simply too much reality for her sensibilities, nor did these scenes in any way approximate the quaint and beguiling portraits of farm life in her books of rhyme. The hens in her Abuela's garden were hideous, the feathers stripped from their thin, exposed necks from the roosters that tore at them constantly. In no way did they resemble the fluffy hens in her picture books. The hierarchy of dominance was always on full display, whether it was a rooster mounting a frightened hen, or her grandfather twisting the head off the rooster that had dared to beak her sister down her thigh leaving a raw, red streak.

That part of the natural world she avoided whenever possible, averted her eyes when she couldn't, and left to her own imagination, eliminated completely. It was this inability to focus on the world as it is that made her quite useless in the household chores her mother set for her and her sisters; the girl was often assigned tasks which would take her aside such as hanging clothes outside on the line where she would take her time serenading the clouds.

Because their family was a large one and one of her sisters very ill, her mother had to often trust the safety of her children to the Lord. Her brother and sister took full advantage of this unbequeathed freedom and were off and away, free as kites, far from home most of the day. Because she was by nature more cautious and easily entertained by her imagination and later her books, the girl kept close to home even when her mother was not watching.

She remembered cold mornings as a very young child when she sat on a little mound of dirt between their home and the church, a patch replete with embedded shards of broken glass, green and amber. For the most part, their sharp edges had been worn smooth by the elements, and so she did not fear picking them up one by one, turning them around in the sun and choosing her favorite jewels. She also loved to straddle the propane pump in their backyard and pretend it was her Pegasus, riding into the start of the evening when her brother made his way home, nor did anyone question or even seem to notice the silvery dust from the pump which rubbed off on her inner thighs.

Another thing she did not like was the perpetual norteño music in her Abuela's home. The frenetically cheerful bars of the accordion, accompanied by the booming and rapid-fire male voices of Spanish radio ads, irritated her severely, yet this soundtrack was ever-present in her childhood as was the scorching humidity and the lusty crowing of the roosters. She could not escape these realities, try as she might.

Chapter 5: Two Brothers

There were two brothers—a poet, and a musician—and when she was old enough to appreciate their story, her father described to her how they would dress formally when they walked the unpaved streets of Los Cedros. The older brother was the poet, the younger a guitarist who played at parties and family functions. Both were renowned for the golden tones they could draw from their instruments—the one from his verses, the other from his cuerdas.

As a woman, she knew that the story of these brothers would be the hardest to believe—she found their story hard to believe—but it was her father recounting the tale and so she delighted in the fact that these two gifted artists had once also called her pueblo home. She loved to imagine them deeply engaged in conversation as they strolled the streets, their starched white shirts pulling them forward like sails, as unaware of their living incongruity as other headlong and dreamy geniuses.

She had hunted down the one book of verse that she could find written by this poet, and was dumbfounded to discover that not only were his lyrics tightly crafted, but they were also full of allusions to Greek mythology and other classical subjects. The poet knew whereof he sang—the banks of his poetry touched other cultures and other times—yet it was rooted, deeply, in the soil of Los Cedros. She discovered that he had followings in Mexico and Spain, and was written about in newspapers of his time. She also discovered a few academic essays about his work from professors at local universities. How many in his pueblo could appreciate his gifts at the time she did not know; his aesthetic was baroque, but with a light touch. He was as full of himself as poets are wont to be, secure that his art, born in this humble pueblo, still had wings to span the Spanish-speaking literary world.

Her father made more mention of his younger brother, the guitarist, who lived in his brother's artistic shadow without envy or resentment. Having embraced the role of accompanist, he gladly followed his older brother's ear all his life. Practicing his melodies alone in his room, or in the company of grateful family and friends, he seemed to have been born with one ear turned toward his instrument, the other to the heavens.

When it was that she first noted the poet's headstone in the camposanto she did not remember, yet how she had ever missed it was the bigger mystery—for there it was, at the very front and center of the assembly: "Aquí yace el Laureado Poeta," the most handsome headstone by far with the engraved noble insignia of lyre and roses.

Chapter 6: Orphan
My father's story

Of his mother, he remembered very little, only the one blurry memory of her making tortillas at the stove. The year he turned four, she was gone, lost to them all in giving birth to his twin younger brothers who died soon after. There were four of them now, three boys and one girl, remaining with their father and his mother and aunts. Like the first bite of winter, their house grew cold.

A year later, when his uncle who often visited with gifts of pan dulce and other treats asked him one day if he would like to come stay with him, he answered, "Yes," imagining it as a choice for a day, a child's evanescent whim.

It was not, however, an invitation to spend the day; it was an open summons to stay forever. As a grown man, he would ask himself, what other answer could I have given as a child of five?

When several weeks went by and his uncle did not respond to his tearful pleas to take him back home, it dawned on him with an anguish he could not name, but felt in his entire body, that he would never return to his brothers and sister. That overwhelming knowledge shook him to the core as if he were being held down and suffocated.

He remembers standing at the railroad tracks that he knew would take him back home, if only he could figure out how to trace his route over the countless miles. Often in his dreams, he stood barefoot and dusty at these tracks, waiting for the sound of the train which would connect all the gaps in his soul, making him whole.

Chapter 7: Return

Much later in life, the woman took an old friend from grad school to visit Los Cedros with the express purpose of introducing her to her pueblo because her friend had never been to the Valley. The woman had also wanted to clean her grandparents' graves and bring flowers. Her father, who had taught her this reverent ritual, had passed away. Because he was not there to do so, she felt called upon as the eldest daughter to take on this sacred duty. She met her friend in Austin and they arrived at Los Cedros on a hot and humid summer day.

The woman was excited to share her village, as if opening up a jewelry box and displaying one after the other of her treasures. She was more than surprised when her friend's first remark was, "Wow, you guys were poor!"

Incredulous at this observation, the woman wheeled upon her asking, "By whose standards?"

"By the world's standards," her friend calmly replied.

With the distance of decades, and almost as if waking up from a dream, the woman then forced herself to see her village through a stranger's eyes. Yes, Los Cedros looked bare and unkempt, as if the intense colors of her childhood had all bled away, leaving only an atmosphere of poverty and limitation.

This particular trip home had already been very unsettling; it had been years since her last visit and so she was accosted by sights she had never before seen: for one, multiple types of law enforcement clustered at the border whereas previously there had only been the Border Patrol. At the entrance to her pueblo, she also saw a strange oblong balloon hanging above the horizon; at first, she stared up at it blankly without the faintest conception of what it could possibly be. The surveillance blimp floated like a menacing starship in an eternal poise, up at the heights where she would lose herself in the shifting cloudscapes and her brother would fly his homemade kites. At her mother's village, she also caught her first glimpse of the Wall with its cruel spikes, like a giant's rusted comb, cutting into the humble fields. Altogether, her part of the world now felt like an occupied territory, a military zone, as if Texas and Washington had finally blown out their birthday candles and converted their violent rhetoric and sinister threats into a flesh and blood dystopia. She felt disoriented, her inner gyroscope desperate to center itself, as her memories collided with this shocking new reality.

She did not feel better until they reached the camposanto where she saw that the graves were still properly festooned with bright plastic flowers. Her grandparents' headstones were at the front of the cemetery by the gate, and grateful for the comfort of ritual, she set upon to wipe them down with water and a rag. She had brought both fresh and plastic bouquets, and setting them in their urns, she stood there quietly, remembering all the happy hours she and her siblings had enjoyed under their care.

As she contemplated, a woman younger than she by perhaps a decade came to stand at her side. The stranger asked what her connection to her Abuelo was, and as she answered, the woman realized that she was in the presence of a relative, not by any recovered name or memory, but by the lilt in her voice and the scent of her skin, like rain. The other woman surely felt the same, as soon upon greeting, they were in each other's arms, holding one another like family. The interlude was intensely sweet, but too soon, the other guest left the cemetery having concluded her own labor of love.

The woman did not want to leave, feeling oddly at peace at a site that used to frighten her as a child. Here, amongst the old names, and the tumbled headstones with chipped azulejos images of saints and angels, she at last felt that she was home.

One more task remained, and that was honoring the grandmother she had never known—her father's mother, her true biological abuela. Because this abuela had so thoroughly disappeared from their family history, she did not remember anyone, even her father, pointing out her grave. Since most of the headstones were marked by name, by process of exclusion she came to the one single grave in the center of the camposanto without a headstone.

She approached her grandmother slowly, as if approaching a beloved stranger, and laid a single red rose on her forlorn grave.

Chapter 8: Dorotea
My grandmother's story

Like many an eager young woman of marriageable age, she had mistaken his goodness of heart for strength of character. They had met in the plaza one afternoon while the small stage for the musicians was being set up. She was with two of her friends, all of them dressed in their long skirts and middy blouses, and he was with his brother and a friend. As was customary, they did not speak at first, largely because the young women strolled the plaza in circles opposite from the young men's. Their universes were separate but intertwined, and their orbits only rarely intersected.

It was his brother who called out to one of her friends, as they had enjoyed a few pleasantries in the past, and asked whether they would be staying for the festivities. She replied yes, and later, when the sun had set and the musicians were playing their first waltz, she got up to dance, leaving Dorotea and their friend alone with the two other young men. Soon, Dorotea's friend also got up to dance and she was left behind with him, a couple by means of reduction.

Dorotea did not mind being in this situation at all. Although she was 20, she had never had a separate conversation with a young man who was not a member of her family, and she was glad that this little twist of fate had brought her into one with the youth she considered the most handsome.

He too was obviously in a novel situation because he found it very hard to speak to her, and every time he dared a question or gave an answer, he blushed. Unlike her, he was fair-skinned, and so his blushes were noticeable, giving her the clue that her fancy was mutual. So she spoke for them both, asking him how he came to be at this dance on a small plaza in Los Cedros.

He was not from the village, but lived with his family in another little pueblo known for its mild men. For so it was that each pueblo, separated by five or ten miles, had distinct personalities and temperaments created by the people who lived there and the various elements of heat, shade, flowers, trees, rocks, and soil.

Her pueblo was marked by fiery impetuous men like her brother Hipólito, and her father, who had only reluctantly allowed his daughter to attend her first dance. She learned that the youth was three years older than she and working in a small grocery store owned by his father. It was his grandfather from Spain who had first settled in the area after the war and his service fighting the Mexicans.

This same war had changed Dorotea's family into foreigners living on their own land as her grandparents had chosen to retain their Mexican citizenship after the treaty which drew their nation's boundary from the Nueces River to the Rio Grande. His grandfather hailed from Castilla and had been enticed to emigrate and join the U.S. Army by promises of land and citizenship; now the family had deepened their roots for a third generation.

She explained to him how she spent her days teaching in the one room schoolhouse around the corner, a profession to which she felt called and loved dearly. For his part, he marveled at this young woman with her vivacious expressions and beautiful eyes, deep and intelligent, shaped like almonds under full half-moon brows. The women in his family worked only in the home and on their small plots of land. He had never been in the presence of such a talkative young woman with a seemingly never-ending stream of interesting things to say.

Their courtship lasted a year, beginning with their first dance weeks later in the same plaza. Within this span of time she was hardly ever alone with him, even in conversation, and these moments were only possible when her friends got up to dance. She didn't meet his family until a few weeks before their wedding in the last week of winter, when the first leaves of the mesquite revealed that the pueblo had survived its last frost.

From a young age, the secret burning desire of her life was to be understood, perhaps because she was not. She was born into a family with a despairing mother and an angry father. Why he was angry was hard to fathom, but she knew that the flames of his anger were lit by his own father who smoldered and raged after the war, or as he referred to it, the Insurrection. She knew that with the changes in borders, their fortunes too had changed drastically. Her father, though uneducated, knew enough about their unjust, degraded status from the stories his father told of "los americanos."

Her brother, being of a reckless "y a mi que?" nature, seemed unperturbed by the emotional undercurrents in their family, and spent many an afternoon out on horseback, carrying on with his friends.

She was different, absorbing all the anger and sadness in her family like a sponge, trying to change the sullen atmosphere with her willful cheerfulness and desire to be of comfort to her parents. It was her decision to become a schoolteacher, and since her profession took nothing from them, as well as kept her away from too early a marriage, her parents grudgingly allowed her to make this choice, the first of her adult life. Her second decision, that of marrying this young man, created much more resistance, especially from her father.

This is what her father saw: his beautiful daughter, quick of mind and fluent of speech, sitting in the parlor with a young man who blushed as often as he spoke, gazing at her with a kind of awe. In short, a perfect mismatch. Nor was this impression sweetened by meeting his parents—a gruff patriarch and his hatchet-faced wife stony with condescension.

Before she even knew what sex could be, the first baby came, a boy sweet-tempered like his father. Then her second son, a dark-complexioned boy with smoldering eyes. Then her daughter, who as an adult could regale a room with stories that engendered peals of laughter, and then their youngest son. The twins whose birth took her life came ten years after her wedding, shortly after she turned thirty-two, nor were these little angels long for the earth after she left them; they survived only a few days.

By the time she had conceived her first child, her entire world had changed. She had left teaching in order to focus more fully on raising a family and her gaiety disappeared soon after. The family she had married into was stern, and fixated on saving money and acquiring land. They had no need for books or music or conversation—in short, all those happy human pastimes which made her, her. She learned to bite her lip and stifle both her laughter and opinions, and her husband, who loved her dearly but never understood her, did not wonder about these changes. Her parents did notice and worried about her, uncharacteristically quiet with her lap full of children. So complete was her transformation that she did not even wonder herself.

They lived in a small house next to her father-in-law's, and she learned to navigate his brusqueness, the way he had of looking at her on the rare occasions his hands were idle. His wife and two sisters were straight-backed women who viewed her with a sort of suspicion, horrified, and not in secret, by her dark complexion and mestizo blood. The facts of her beauty and grace were completely lost on them since they did not measure the world by external vanities. They owned only one book, an old cracked leather Bible, which they had brought from Spain.

The language of proper respect was far more important to them than the language of letters and numbers. Accordingly, the children were kept home to be educated by their mother, with the design of, as soon as possible, being put to some useful work. The day she passed away, only her husband wept. The women looked around at the room full of silent children and two tiny infants wrapped together in a cradle. They would keep them all together if they could, but if fate were to bring some relative forward with an offer to take one of them, they would also be open to that.

From Heaven, she looked down and saw the little village laid out like a game, each character playing out his or her role. She saw her children grow, and one day, her oldest son stopped asking when she was coming back. She saw her brother come by their house and take her second son away, as he was of an age where he would not understand what was happening, and the women had assessed that his pain would be the least. She saw them all grow up, and then her granddaughters and grandsons come into the world, and then their own children.

As the years went by and her adult grandchildren would infrequently visit the cemetery and lay flowers at her brother's grave, she yearned to call out to them, to look them in the eyes and take them into her arms.

"I'm here," she would whisper, "your family as well, although only a fragment of a memory will be attached to my name."

Over the long years, she yearned in vain for them to turn around and walk over to the unmarked place where she slept, and to sit with her a while and tell her about the world.

Chapter 9: Boy
My brother's story

Later he told her, "I was a brute, a beast, but you don't know who my teachers were."

From the age of five onward, the village was his kingdom. He would rise every morning to explore it, not returning home until their mother called out his name as the first stars pricked the evening sky. He doesn't remember taking food with him on his forays, or even water, sustained by the very air of adventure. His companion in these jaunts was his friend down the street, the boy with a raggedy Caesar haircut. His own head was shaved clean, like a Shaolin monk.

At the beginning, their adventures were harmless or at least largely so: sword fights with weapons carved out of orange crates, games of cowboys and Indians, kites made of newspapers on crosses of thin bamboo, their long tails knotted with colored rags and launched in the plaza. How high the kites flew above the church bell tower, carried by gusts of wind, until they disappeared from sight almost entirely in the bright blue sky! Rubber band fights, tops, yo-yos, his moments were perpetual action slowed only by a new passing fancy. The harm came mostly to the poor creatures they managed to capture. The chicharras they flew on a string or impaled on a mesquite thorn. The black and red ants they forced to fight, lured by a cunning trail of Vienna sausage. The sparrows that tumbled from the trees when, at last, he received the gift of a BB gun at the age of nine from his Abuelo.

But there was also the harm they drew to themselves though miraculously never succumbed to—running fleetly along the banks of the river, banks which dropped at a 45-degree angle to the seemingly placid waters, but the river was deep and had a stiff undertow. From time to time, they watched a fisherman pull out the alarming alligator gars, heavy and thrashing, their long, pointed snouts lined with razor-sharp teeth. They played for hours in the lagoon running along the riverbanks, the same shrouded place where la Llorona was said to wander in the evening at just the same time their mothers' voices called them in for dinner, their names hanging in the air.

"The loneliest year of my life," he recounted, "was the year my best friend entered school."

"Se fue para la escuela," his friend's mother called out to him as he stood on the porch, his face and hands pressed against the dusty screen door.

Years later, he became the youngest member of an older group of boys, and there the tutelage—which flew against everything he learned at home, school, and church—began in earnest, a tutelage which was as severe and inescapable as it was randomly violent.

"The things we said, the things we did," he confessed to her, his voice dropping to a whisper.

The only veiled glimpse, for example, he dared give her about their self-styled fight clubs was the moment they all dreaded yet stoically endured, the fingers pointing imperiously in their direction: "You!"

"¡Niño travieso!" Abuela scolded him in exasperation, "¡Manos de lumbre, manos de hierro!" For there was always something in his hands, and generally, he was tearing it apart. Once, he beheaded a whole flock of chickens. Once, he created a human bridge with his strong little torso by hanging between their sofa and a chair, only to fall on his younger sister and break her two front teeth. Once, he almost hit his younger brother with a ricocheting BB gun pellet. Blood did not faze him, as did little else, and he came home each evening sun baked and sweaty, with halos of cobwebs in his hair and necklaces of dirt around his neck.

Some of their stories matched, others did not, revealing an unexpected facet of personality about the adults who raised them. They both did remember, for example, the day Abuelo stood in the street with his belt hanging from his hand, waiting to confront him and their sister who was his happy accomplice in crime. Neither remembered whether Abuelo had indeed followed through with this threat to punish them; the possibility alone had been sufficient terror and forced them to separately bury the final act.

"He had a double-banded Ranger belt," her brother explained, unlike her, alive to external detail from an early age. She did not know that once he saw Abuelo put a small toy in his pants pocket when they were out shopping (why?), the same kind of toy he would sometimes present to them. Or that Abuelo had taken away the new football his uncle had given him, and regifted it to a group of poor boys in the village. Nor did she remember that Margarita was a snorer, and that when she fell asleep, he waited for that gentle rumble to commence his escape. Equally unlike her, he remembered family and friends in the village—first names and surnames—how they were connected, what kinds of jobs his friends' fathers had had, and what their childhood friends were doing now as adults. He was committed to visiting and cultivating this web of human connections in Los Cedros, activities she would never be able to do even if she wanted to having lost the thread of their interlaced stories long ago.

"You and I had very different childhoods," he once quietly mused to her. Then he added a statement that cut her to her core, all the broken treasures of their lives between them: "I wish you had been happy like me—I was free!"

Chapter 10: Fidencio Díaz
Veteran, teacher

Even after a decade in the classroom, the questions from the new white teachers remained the same.

"Why do you speak English?"
"I'm an American citizen."

"How did you become a teacher?"
"I went to college."

"How did you get to college?"
"On the GI Bill."

On the next question, he would always pause, not because he did not know the answer, but because he did not know the questioner.

"Why did you decide to teach history?"
As a rule, he would dryly respond, "Because it repeats itself."

When he first started teaching at the high school, there were only a handful of fellow Mexican-American teachers. By the time he retired thirty years later, Mexican-American teachers predominated.

To the girl and her brothers and sisters he was a portly, formal man sparing of conversation, although genial to them and to their father, who was nearly ten years his junior and also a veteran and a teacher. Mr. Díaz had served in World War II, their father in Korea. Neither man had seen combat, which was a blessing, because neither had the temperament for war, especially for death from their own hands. Their wartime experiences, of which they rarely spoke, bonded them: the fact that their lives had been shaped by war, but not destroyed by it, and the fact that they had had the opportunity to see a slice of the world via their service. These experiences had expanded and sharpened their minds, and even better, had qualified them to receive the key to a better life: a university education.

A few of Mr. Díaz' older cousins had enlisted, taking the train to San Antonio with nothing but a few coins in their pockets. He, on the other hand, was drafted at 18 but successfully postponed his enlistment until after his high school graduation. The reason for his deferred status was the fact that he was the only son of his widowed mother, a woman who, having received no formal education whatsoever, still signed her name with an "X." Late in her life when her faculties began to fail, her doctor had handed the permission for surgery to Mr. Díaz, only to have his mother snatch the form from the doctor's hand in anger. "¡Yo firmo aquí!" she exclaimed, and then scrawled her X. The children were a bit intimidated by this wrinkled but spry woman who enjoyed smoking hand-rolled Bugler tobacco cigarettes. She seemed a world apart from her professional son with his starched shirts and slacks and his even-tempered speech. In many ways, she was.

His keenly observant nature and calm temperament were evident from his very earliest days in elementary school. Although he only heard and spoke Spanish at home, he quickly learned English, noting that his above grade reading and writing skills protected him from the whimsical wrath of his young white teachers with their tight curls and tighter smiles. He knew that he was poor, and that his teachers hated the Spanish language and Mexican children. He accepted these facts with all the dispassion a seven-year-old could muster, wise enough to know that neither tears nor struggle were fruitful, or indeed, options.

He took, instead, the road of quiet compliance, focusing on the means of their torture and his liberation: the words themselves. He was perhaps in the fifth grade when he realized that there was a sure, if invisible, bridge of mutual understanding between him and the writers of the stories he discovered on his own in the school's threadbare library: a bridge which, if his teachers had ever walked, they had walked quickly and with their collars up. He was keenly aware of their intellectual and moral limitations; his survival depended upon it. A few grades later, he blossomed into the sardonic thinker he was to be for the rest of his life. Having suffered fools and possessing no power to constrain them, he had by way of compensation learned to study the foolish closely, categorizing them by their feints and follies.

By the time he was in high school, this long practice of intense but quiet observation had formed an aura around him which even the most racist of his teachers dared not penetrate. Privately, they whispered and plotted against him, but their subterfuges were of no potency against this subtle young man, determined to prevail over them through fidelity to his studies. He knew that they could not fathom him, and so he continued to grow undisturbed as a reader, writer, and thinker, like the cedar that furtively commandeered drops of water for ten acres, joining with other cedars and creating a secret network of powerful roots.

He knew who he was, and who they were. For their part, he was that most implacable of foes: a smart Mexican.

Of his service in the War he spoke very little for in truth, he carried a great deal of survivor guilt. Fairly quickly, his superior writing skills attracted the attention of one of his commanding officers, and after basic training he found himself assigned to the public relations department where his job was to write press releases for the news outlets back in the States. In cool, dispassionate prose, he wrote about the storming of Normandy; he wrote about the challenges of the Pacific theater; he wrote about the liberation of the Nazi death camps. When he returned to Los Cedros, he discovered that one of his cousins had been killed in France, and that two of his boyhood friends had lost their lives in the Pacific.

He understood the equivalence of things: why the war was just, yet unimaginably tragic. What he did not know is whether it was fate or God Himself who chose the soldiers who were to return, and those who would not. He remained a man of faith to the end of his days—a faith fostered mainly by the goodness of the men with whom he had served. His faith acknowledged—and endured—the cruelty he had known of the world—both through the depravity of war, as well as through the dangers of being born in a dark brown skin at this time of the eternally bloody U.S.-Mexico farce.

After the war, he enrolled at the University of Texas at Austin. There were only a handful of fellow Mexican-American students, so they had no choice but to become great friends. He chose to major in History because, having just lived through a war he helped report, he was curious as to which stories made it into the final accounting of textbooks. He knew that history was written by the winners; no one growing up on the Texas border would ever assume otherwise.

He was fascinated by the periods in history when intellectual discourse began to ignite the brush fires which would eventually burst forth into full-fledged rebellion. He studied the American, French and Mexican Revolutions, and was equally stimulated by the ideas of Jefferson, Rousseau, and Flores Magón.

He had never felt freer or more himself than during those four years at university. The fact that he was a veteran protected him in ways that were new, for before the war, there were even fewer Mexican-Americans enrolled in Texas colleges and universities. He felt not exactly welcomed, but secure enough with his cadre of friends and the occasional sympathetic professor. Continuing his boyhood obsession with reading, he spent hundreds of hours alone in the library stacks. He had a monastic temperament and disciplined mind; after college, he returned home to take care of his mother and never married.

As a high school teacher, he had seen it all: tragicomic scenes from the continuous replay of the conquest of Mexico, South Texas edition. He was surrounded by teachers who snickered at the Mexican-American students' poor English skills, or shoddy clothes, or even their smell.

"You can't wash off the stink of the onion fields," one red-faced teacher quipped at lunch one day.

"No, you sure can't," another responded in her lazy, pointed drawl, her thin triangular eyebrows peaked like tents. And so on and so forth.

You might have guessed that these teachers had been educated at the Ivies to see in what a self-satisfied manner they sauntered the hallways and spoke up at meetings. Their fixed ideas about the students they taught were, to their minds, never too often repeated: how ignorant these parents were to pluck their children out of school to work in the fields. What kind of morals were being taught in the home to have daughters pregnant at 16? What a wild boy that

Enrique was, to drop out of school rather than to be thrashed for the umpteenth time.

The fact that they themselves were one generation away from the fields—if that—was lost on them. Possessing no self-reflection, they were not capable of enjoying the delicious meat of irony. He, however, relished the feast and said nothing during these noon gatherings of chachalacas, choosing instead to read his newspaper and sit alone in a corner of the faculty lounge.

He was not amused by their buffoonery, but never took pains to challenge them as he did not view them as worthy opponents; moreover, he knew himself to be vastly outnumbered. Not the Spartan 300 showed greater fortitude than Mr. Díaz having endured 30 years in the faculty lounge without throwing a single punch or filing a lawsuit.

Although not an overtly religious man, the world had cured him of that, the one act of devotion Mr. Díaz was sure to observe in any church he visited was to pray at the inevitable Shrine of Fallen Heroes, the niche always to be found in some dark corner, generally at the feet the Virgin, of all the local boys and men who had either served or lost their lives in any one of a succession of American wars.

It was there, before the photographs of soldiers in their freshly pressed uniforms, that he found his closest communion. There was always a framed grove of photos, glittering because of the votives lit by mothers, and tías, and sisters, and daughters. The reflections from the candles made it easier for him to greet his comrades' trusting faces, most of them in the first blush of manhood. It was hard for him to kneel there bearing witness, but harder still for him not to. As a veteran, as a teacher, he could never turn away from their raised hands, their endless questions.

Chapter 11: Foreign Queen
My mother's story

Though her own pueblo was only ten miles away, it was a different kingdom entirely, or rather, a queendom, since her pueblo was a matriarchy and her mother its reigning matriarch. Los Cedros, on the other hand, was always at high noon, and her father-in-law, the children's grandfather, its chieftain. Whereas her pueblo was magically green and fertile, a throng of pink-blossomed corona vines cascading over and through the simple chain link fence which marked her mother's home, Los Cedros was dramatically stark, the sunlight blistering off the caliche on the street outside her new home.

As much as any young woman could prepare for marriage, she had prepared. Coming of age in the '50s, she had taken home economics and knew how to bake fresh yellow cakes with mounds of seven-minute frosting piled high as the cumulus clouds drifting above her head. She also knew how to make patties from tinned salmon and cabbage salad dressed with lemon juice, and how to sew on the dainty sewing machine given to her by her mother as a wedding gift. She was educated too, having recently graduated from the local university, and had found a job to teach at a nearby elementary school.

She was extroverted and well-rounded; in high school she had played basketball and the trombone. She had also been a cheerleader, leaning back flirtatiously in her uniform in the photo that her children loved to gaze at as adults. She was the middle girl of a happy family of six: three girls and three boys. Her father was much older than her mother, and worked as a foreman on a tract of orchards. With her and her siblings, he was always gentle, bringing home bags of oranges or pasteles. Soft-spoken and encouraging, after a long day in the hot sun he would embrace them as he rested on the porch, holding them close. As an adolescent, her emotional life was idyllic, unperturbed by anything more serious than getting her hair to curl just so or choosing the right shade of lipstick.

She had worked in the fields for a few summers before the miracle of a college education appeared at her door like the Angel Gabriel.

She had imagined that, like other girls, she would at best work as a bank teller after graduation, but one day a white man visited her high school offering modest college scholarships for those bold enough to say "Yes." She said "Yes," and whatever daring the children developed later in life, they attributed to her. Their father's counsel, on the other hand, was always for them to recognize and stay within their limits. She was the adventurer, the one longing to take her risks, and so she had also said "Yes" to their father's marriage proposal.

Why she chose him was not hard to understand: he was charming and handsome and just returned from the war in his crisp uniform. Only a few years older than she, he was already enrolled at another university and came home for the summers. They met at a dance in the same plaza where his own mother and father had met. Their fates subsequently intertwined at many such dances, and then, within a year, they became engaged. Young men and women were so serious then, even in their early 20s, eager for the responsibility of marriage and starting a family. Later, as an adult, it struck the girl with some amazement to fully comprehend that her parents had married *in order* to have children; no cart before a horse in this generation. The strictures of Catholicism and the expectations of their families, together with a morally conservative national climate, made the choice as to what to do with one's life more readily apparent, nor could one characterize their choices as narrow. Starting a family and entering their professions, in both cases, teaching, was as grand an adventure for them as the girl later leaving for college in California and traveling to study abroad in Spain.

Possessing a mild and steadfast temperament, her mother accepted the changes married life brought in cheerful stride. There were her in-laws across the street, with opinions on everything based on nothing; that was a change. Another major change were the babies that came one after the other, filling her days with hours of changing diapers, and cooking, and washing clothes to hang out in the sunshine. She was the type of mother who cooed to all her babies, and knew how to make them feel snug and secure, expertly comforting their childhood fears and bandaging their bloody knees. She spent decades on the duties inherent in raising a large family, punctuated with occasional meta-crises such as hurricanes, a houseful of children with the chicken pox, and a daughter born with a congenital heart defect. Her love, strength, and intelligence saw them all through, and she kept her own beauty and sanity intact, reigning as a sweet and attentive queen over their lives. The girls' hair was always brushed, and pulled up in pigtails and bows. Their dresses were lovely, and even when handsewn, stylish. They properly observed the rites of Baptism, Confirmation, and First Communion, and their immunizations were all up to date. Not only was she a loving mother, but she was also a dedicated teacher to hundreds of Mexican children who flocked to her as a kind oasis in their often very difficult lives.

The one change which startled her, and which she found difficult to accept from the very beginning, was her husband's weekly foray to the pool hall down the street, generally on Saturday nights, and generally to ill avail. The first time he came home drunk, their firstborn already asleep, she felt fear for the first time in her life. Nothing in her happy childhood or adolescence could have prepared her for her husband's stumbling gait or slurred, aggressive speech. Alarmed, she had turned to her mother, who advised her to keep silent and accept this as the way of men.

She did keep silent for the first year, saying nothing again to her mother and stopping herself from sharing her confusion and frustration with her sisters and married friends. As more babies came and his behavior continued, she began resentfully stopping him at the front door, beseeching him to not wake the children. Later still, when her oldest children were in elementary school, sparks of real anger exploded from her quiet soul, and they had weekly fights over the car keys or one last drink. Years later, she felt reoccurring cycles of hopeless sorrow and icy rage, until, the children all grown and gone, she was left to live with him in loneliness and suspicion.

More than marriage itself, or motherhood, or serving as a teacher for decades, this secret thread of her life transformed her and became her own wrestling with the angel. Amongst her life's many blessings, including this same man who found sobriety and faithfully took care of her at the end of her life when she needed him the most, her spirit had also come to understand the cruel fate of living as a foreign queen in your own home.

Chapter 12: Los Cedros
My pueblo's story

After the Spanish came, the river was always red with blood. The girl would not have known this, so sheltered and protected was she by her parents and whitewashed education. Until she was an adult woman, she would not understand the true heritage of this place she called home. The Spanish, lured irresistibly by land and gold, came with their horses and oxen and heavy carts and rough men and priests craving the souls of converts. That went on for centuries until the American troops crossed the river to fight the Mexicans all the way to the Capital. Then came Prohibition when the narrow river separating the two nations was rife with illicit runs for tequila. There were also the recurring natural disasters like Hurricane Beulah, when the river completely overflowed its banks and the people had to return to the pueblo on boats. There were always traffickers associated with this part of the world: drug traffickers, human traffickers, *coyotes*. The river was always red, but the children did not know this.

In her earlier days, there was only one type of law enforcement at the river—the Border Patrol—tall, red-faced men wearing sunglass visors who moved with a deathly calm. How surprised she was once when her sweet-tempered mother referred to them as "rinches." By her mother's twinkling eyes, she knew that she was jesting in that subtle way that communicates on several levels, but still.

Gringos, gabachos, bolillos. She had heard these words in the village, but they did not make any particular sense to her. Nor did her father's oft-repeated refrain "Never hate anybody because of their race" make any more sense because, outside of the Border Patrol, her pueblo was exclusively Mexican.

She felt a vague fear in the Border Patrol's presence the few times her path had crossed theirs. There was no family story that pointed them out as villains, but still these pejoratives rang in her ears. She attributed her fear of them to the fact that her Abuelo hunted white-winged doves outside the state-sanctioned fall season when the men of Los Cedros rented their fields to Anglo hunters with their licenses and permits. Bloody sacks of felled birds. Yes, that was the danger.

The village had always known what she did not or could not comprehend: the violence which framed her idyllic world, and how everlasting that violence was, and the human misery without end. The poor who lived in Los Cedros, and the desperately poor who swam across the river in the dead of night for the chance at a life less bleak. The village knew all the waves of ownership and succession, all the changing flags that dictated the life of the frontera; knew the good and evil men and women who had passed through or stayed to lay roots; knew the greed and lust and hatred which were as much a part of it as the blue skies or caliche road; knew the seasons of plenty and seasons of drought, times when the plazas were merry with dancing or baseball games, and times when the entire village drew in on itself in grief and exhaustion.

As for sentinels, Los Cedros had always relied on the trees, which here were more akin to guardian spirits and fierce protectors of the land and people. The ebonies, with their dark, indestructible wood; the anacuas, with their dense leaves abrasive like sandpaper; the mesquite, with their maze of wicked thorns; and the cedar, with their roots reaching deep into the earth and spreading out half the size of a football field. One cedar, then another along the bank, amassing their salty needles and making it impossible at times for the Border Patrol to find the men and women who hid with thunderous hearts.

Yes, through eras of drought and plenty, the village had always found its way, but now, there was something different—a war that had left it anesthetized and weak, a war announced by the advent of the surveillance balloons floating lazily above the fields. The balloons were a Cyclops which never slept, splitting each moment into hundreds of photographs that recorded every miniscule detail for miles and miles: the quivering whiskers of the jackrabbit standing on its hind legs in the same field she had helped her Abuelo hunt at dusk. The Cyclops which detected everything and perceived nothing: for example, the exact coordinates at which the young mother drowned with her baby.

The era of the surveillance balloons and winged drones was orchestrated by well-heeled politicians in San Francisco and DC, whose shoes never betrayed a speck of dust, and whose voices never ascended beyond a comfortable pearl-like luster, bemoaning this and that, and promising vigilance through technology. Sentiments spoken to other well-heeled people in San Francisco and DC in rooms with soft carpets and deep chairs and high windows letting in the West or East Coast sun, where the wine was served discreetly, and the glimmer of pearls sent out their quiet messages of polished educations and the tranquil intertwining of generations.

Technology was to be the new clean solution to the bloody violence of the river and it promised no violence at all: merely blind ogling every hour of the day, every day of the year, draining the heavens of their vibrancy and the fields of their luster. That no such leader in San Francisco or DC would allow, for even a second, these soul-sucking demons to fly over their stately mansions where their grandbabies slept in profound peace was a given. No, the clean technological solution was for the brown people who died at the river like cattle.

For the first time in its history, her pueblo needed someone to remember its stories and to entrust them to a space-time capsule impervious to injury and infamy. It needed to escape the death trance of the balloons, strung like pearls above the river, and the now half a dozen types of law enforcement with their weapons of war and headlights piercing the night.

Her pueblo needed someone to call back and safeguard its spirit before it slipped into oblivion and nothing again would ever make sense. It needed someone to speak it into safety: *un diamante cerrado,* a closed diamond. That last bit of magic, loaded like a rain cloud, was what her pueblo needed to survive: someone to honor and proudly claim it; someone to surround it with an impenetrable seal of love; someone to connect its stories like the roots of the cedar, desperately seeking the river.

Study Guide

Dear Students:

I have written this study guide to help you better understand and remember the text; to help you connect the text with your own personal experience; to spark further study on historical contexts and related topics; and to encourage you to expand your vocabulary.

Questions for Review:

To understand and remember what you are reading in each chapter, you will need to read it at least two and preferably three times. The first time you read a chapter, allow yourself to read it for pleasure and to enjoy how a character's story unfolds. This first reading can be quick—like gazing out of the window on a car ride and watching the flashing scenery. The second time you read a chapter, I suggest you slow down and read with more concentration, like getting out of the car and taking a walk to explore the terrain. Before you read a second time, you might refer to the Questions for Review to see what the main questions are that you should be able to answer. Reading the chapter a third time will help you absorb and retain all the new information you have learned.

Personal Reflection:

This section encourages you to connect your own personal experience with the experiences of the characters in each chapter. Reflecting upon your own experience is a good way to see where you and the characters have similar or different perspectives. The goal of writing is to get you to think for yourself, so personal reflection is key. You may use this section to explore your thoughts and feelings in your own writing.

For Further Study:

In this section, I invite you to do additional research into the historical contexts for each chapter, as well as to investigate related social issues. I have especially highlighted research areas concerning Mexican-American/Chicano history since much of that history is buried.

Words to Check Out!:

Building your vocabulary will help you further your mastery of a language—in this case English—and thereby greatly expand what you can understand and express. In this section, I have highlighted words from each chapter with which you may not be familiar and invite you to look up their definitions. It may take some practice to learn to use these new words in your own speech or writing, but with effort you can learn a few new words at a time. Did you feel "good" or "elated" after your long run? The words you use make a difference!

Chapter 1: Father Ávila, *Activist Priest*

Questions for review:
1. How does Father Ávila's appearance suggest his purpose in life?
2. How do people respond to Father Ávila? What is his effect on others?
3. What is the nature of the conflict between Father Ávila and the Bishop?
4. How was Father Ávila's congregation in Los Cedros different from the one in San Antonio?
5. How did Father Ávila feel about being transferred to Los Cedros? Did his feelings change?
6. What kind of pleasures did Father Ávila enjoy? What were his "little vanities?"
7. What did Father Ávila demand of his parishioners?
8. Why did Father Ávila participate in the farm workers' march? Why do you think he chose to wear red on that day?

Personal reflection:
1. Are there spiritual, political, community, or school leaders who you respect and admire? Why do you respect and admire them?
2. What makes them inspiring?
3. Have you ever had to stand up for your beliefs in the face of opposition? What was that experience like for you? Did you have allies?

For further study:
1. César Chávez, Dolores Huerta, Larry Itliong and the founding of the United Farm Workers (UFW) labor movement (1962),
2. The Delano Grape Strike in California (1965-1970).
3. The UFW Rio Grande City Strike and March to Austin, Texas (1966).
4. Role of the U.S. Catholic Bishops in generating public support for César Chávez and the UFW movement.
5. Ongoing challenges for farm workers including during the Covid-19 pandemic.
6. The Chicano Civil Rights Movement (Also known as "El Movimiento," 1940s-1970s and ongoing).

Words to check out!

- jutting
- flecks
- luminous
- ruddy
- mundane
- sensual
- cassock
- sweltering
- jovial
- engendered
- grandeur
- bedecked
- beseeching
- rationale
- orator
- sundial
- charisma
- radiated
- hinterlands
- perimeter
- conservative
- sacristy
- vestments
- piercing
- acumen
- fraction
- vanities
- partaken
- cuisine
- chasuble
- doilies
- paltry
- manna
- vigilant
- itinerant
- flanked
- tapestry

Chapter 2: Margarita, *Caregiver*

Questions for review:
1. Describe Margarita's life. Who are the many people for whom she is responsible?
2. How does Margarita cope with her duties and obligations?
3. How do the children feel about Margarita? How do they treat her?
4. How is Margarita feeling when she experiences a heart attack?

Personal reflection:
1. Have you ever known someone like Margarita whose life was all about giving? What kind of interactions did you have with her or him?
2. Do you have experience as a caregiver in your family or community? What is that experience like for you?

For further study:
1. The Catholic Church's ideas about the role of women in services, including in the role of priests.
2. The challenges for long-term caregivers.
3. Health outcomes and disparities for Latinas in the U.S.

Words to check out!
- unassuming
- parasols
- stature
- gingham
- decipher
- prone
- forays
- brake
- chastened
- impish
- extract
- constituted
- chalice
- matriarchal
- vessels
- scalloped

Chapter 3: Doña Isabel, *Curandera*

Questions for review:

1. What do the children of Los Cedros think about Doña Isabel? What about her contributes to their beliefs?
2. What does Doña Isabel's home reveal about her life?
3. How does the girl respond to accidently witnessing Doña Isabel performing a spiritual "limpia?"
4. What does Father Ávila think about Doña Isabel? How are they similar? Different?

Personal reflection:

1. Do you know of someone like Doña Isabel who practices as a traditional healer? How are they perceived by the people they help and the community?
2. Have you ever gone to a curandera/o or experienced Ayurveda or Traditional Chinese Medicine (including acupuncture)? What was your experience like?

For further study:

1. Don Pedro Jaramillo, Curandero; also known as "The Healer of Los Olmos" and "The Saint of Falfurrias," South Texas (1829-1907).
2. Curanderismo, Ayurveda, Traditional Chinese Medicine and other non-Western/holistic/traditional practices of medicine.

Words to check out!

- unfathomably
- votive
- disconcerting
- comprehension
- portal
- vocation
- fidelity
- dubious
- exceedingly

Chapter 4: Girl, *My story*

Questions for review:
1. What does the girl think and feel about her village? What are the most important places for her?
2. What aspects of Los Cedros are lost on the girl? Why?
3. What are the girl's strengths? How do her strengths prepare her to tell her pueblo's story?
4. What are the places and activities that the girl most loves? Why?
5. What does the girl's belief that there are "blue hollyhocks" reveal about her?
6. What is the girl's family life like? How does she feel about her father and mother?
7. How does the girl discover fairytales and poetry? What is the effect on her of that discovery?
8. What is the girl's experience of school?
9. What were her Abuelo and Abuela like? How does she feel about them?
10. Why does her Abuelo threaten to send the children to Monterrey, Mexico?
11. How do adults respond to the girl?
12. What are the parts of her life in Los Cedros that the girl does not like?

Personal reflection:
1. What is your birth order in your family? Are you the oldest, middle, youngest, or only child? How does that status affect you?
2. What kind of relationship do you have with your grandparents or other important older adults? How do you get along with them?
3. Have you ever experienced feeling like an outsider at your school? Why? How did you cope and adapt?

For further study:
1. Psychological impact of racism on a child's development.
2. Impact of first language suppression on the development of a child's self-esteem.
3. Theories of bilingual education and the optimal way to develop second language competence.
4. Intellectual and social benefits of bilingualism.

Words to check out!

- iridescent
- circumscribed
- perch
- slumbering
- Cerberus
- vapors
- luxuriant
- demarcated
- oblong
- stark
- startling
- prohibited
- exiled
- temperamental
- fidelity
- nary
- indelibly
- deciphered
- pavilions
- coax
- captivated
- nascent
- ensconce
- entranced
- throng
- azure
- apex
- radius
- alluring
- fatal
- indignation
- rapt
- arrested
- dislodged
- estranged
- phantasm
- concocted
- fissure
- psyche

- consciousness
- divined
- potency
- sorcery
- gilt
- bewitched
- fanciful
- stern
- unconsciously
- splaying
- rhinestone
- restrained
- savory
- beguiling
- glaucoma
- cipher
- reckoned
- fetch
- native
- bias
- righteously
- vigilant
- ironclad
- sauntered
- resolute
- impertinent
- paradox
- approximate
- quaint
- averting
- unbequeathed
- embedded
- perpetual
- frenetically

Chapter 5: Two Brothers

Questions for review:
1. For which talents are these brothers recognized? Why does the woman appreciate them?
2. "Their starched white shirts pulling them forward like sails," what does this description reveal about the personalities of the brothers?
3. Why does the woman describe them as a "living incongruity?"
4. How well was the poet known in his day? How does his guitarist brother feel about his older brother's fame?
5. What does the poet's headstone in the village cemetery reveal about his self-image?

Personal reflection:
1. Do you know of people from your town, city or community who have achieved recognition? Why are they celebrated?
2. Do you have a sibling, cousin, or friend with whom you are very close? What draws you together?
3. Do you practice an art form that you enjoy? Why do you enjoy it?

For further study:
Chicano literary classics: Oscar "Zeta" Acosta, *Autobiography of a Brown Buffalo*; Rudolfo Anaya, *Bless Me, Última*; Gloria Anzaldúa, *Borderlands/La Frontera: The New Mestiza*; Ana Castillo, *Massacre of the Dreamers: Essays on Xicanisma*; Sandra Cisneros, *The House on Mango Street*; Alicia Gaspar de Alba, *Sor Juana's Second Dream*; Rolando Hinojosa, *Estampas del Valle*; Cherríe Moraga, *Loving in the War Years*; Estella Portillo-Trambley, *Rain of Scorpions and Other Writings*; Tomás Rivera, *y no se lo tragó la tierra/And the Earth Did Not Devour Him*; Luis J. Rodriguez, *Always Running: La Vida Loca: Gang Days in L.A.* ; Luis Alberto Urrea, *The Hummingbird's Daughter*; Victor Villaseñor, *Rain of Gold*; Helena María Viramontes, *The Moths and Other Stories*.

Chicano literary classics (poetry): Francisco X. Alarcón, *Snake Poems: An Aztec Incantation*; Alurista, *Floricanto en Aztlán*; Jimmy Santiago Baca, *Immigrants in Our Own Land*; Ana Castillo, *Women Are Not Roses*; Lorna Dee Cervantes, *Emplumada*; Sandra Cisneros, *My Wicked Wicked Ways*; Lucha Corpi, *Palabras de mediodía/Noon Words*; Ray González, *The Heat of Arrivals*; Rodolfo "Corky" González, *I am Joaquín*; Juan

Felipe Herrera, *Border-Crosser with a Lamborghini Dream*; Ángela de Hoyos, *Arise, Chicano! and Other Poems*; Demetria Martínez, *Breathing Between the Lines: Poems*; José Montoya, *El sol y los de abajo (The Sun and Below) and Other R.C.A.F. Poems*; Pat Mora, *Adobe Odes*; Alberto Ríos, *Whispering to Fool the Wind*; Gary Soto, *The Elements of San Joaquín*; Carmen Tafolla, *This River Here: Poems of San Antonio*; Alma Luz Villanueva, *Planet with Mother, May I?*; Tino Villanueva, *Hay Otra Voz: Poems*; Bernice Zamora, *Restless Serpents*.

Note: These authors and titles represent a sampling of the scope and diversity of Chicano literary classics; many of the writers and poets listed here have written several books across different genres. Other areas for fruitful further study include younger generations of Chicano writers as well as artistic achievements by Chicanos in the visual and performing arts including drawing, painting, printmaking, sculpture, photography, singing, spoken word, music, stand-up comedy, theater, and film.

Words to check out!
- renowned
- incongruity
- headlong
- dumbfounded
- allusions
- lyric
- aesthetic
- baroque
- wont
- Poet Laureate
- engraved
- insignia
- lyre

Chapter 6: Orphan, *My father's story*

Questions for review:
1. What does the girl's father remember about his mother? How old was he when she died?
2. Why did her father say "yes" to living with his uncle? Did he regret his decision?
3. Why did her father dream of standing by the railroad tracks?
4. How does her father's childhood affect him as an adult?

Personal reflection:
1. What was your father's or other important male figure's childhood like? How did his early experiences affect his later years?
2. Did you or someone you know experience early childhood trauma? How did you or they learn to cope?

For further study:
1. The connection between early childhood trauma and substance use.
2. The importance of stable relationships with parents or other primary caregivers in early child development (attachment theory).

Words to check out!
- evanescent
- summons
- anguish
- route

Chapter 7: Return

Questions for review:
1. Why is the woman visiting Los Cedros? Who is accompanying her? What does she want to share with her friend?
2. Why is she surprised when her friend describes Los Cedros as "poor?" How does this statement affect the woman?
3. What new developments in Los Cedros does the woman see on this visit that confuse and unsettle her?
4. Why does the woman feel better in the cemetery? Who does she meet? How does she know that she is in the presence of "family?"
5. How does the woman find her biological grandmother's grave? How does she honor this abuela?

Personal reflection:
1. Have you ever gone back to visit a place you really used to love and seen how much it has changed? How did it change?
2. How do you, your family, or community honor people who have died? What are your mourning rituals?

For further study:
1. Surveillance along the U.S.-Mexico border; effects on asylum seekers and residents; issues of privacy and civil liberties.
2. History of the U.S.-Mexico Wall; effects on asylum seekers and residents; legal challenges; ecological consequences.
3. History of the U.S. Border Patrol; allegations of abuse including use of excessive force.

Words to check out!
- express
- reverent
- incredulous
- wheeled
- unkempt
- limitation
- unsettling
- accosted
- clustered
- conception
- menacing

- poise
- occupied
- converted
- rhetoric
- sinister
- dystopia
- gyroscope
- festooned
- urns
- recovered
- interlude
- azulejos
- biological
- exclusion
- forlorn

Chapter 8: Dorotea, *My grandmother's story*

Questions for review:
1. How well does Dorotea know her fiancé before they marry? How is her personality different from his?
2. How does Dorotea's family history differ from her fiancé's? How do those differences create potential conflict?
3. What are their families like?
4. What do they think of one another?
5. How does becoming a wife and mother change Dorotea?
6. How does Dorotea's death affect her family?

Personal reflection:
1. What were your grandparents like as young people? How did they meet and marry?
2. Have you known married couples from very different families or cultures?
3. Has your family experienced a historical tragedy? How did it affect them?

For further study:
1. The U.S.-Mexican War (also known as the Mexican-American War, 1846-1848) and the Treaty of Guadalupe Hidalgo.
2. The U.S. justification for the War; perspectives from American political leaders including James K. Polk, Ulysses S. Grant, and Abraham Lincoln. The idea of "Manifest Destiny."
3. How Mexico in the 1800s differed from the United States in beliefs about the legality of slavery. How the outcome of the U.S.-Mexico War led to the conditions for the American Civil War (1861-1865).

Words to check out!
- middy
- customary
- intertwined
- intersected
- pleasantries
- reduction
- novel
- fancy

- mutual
- impetuous
- enticed
- emigrate
- vivacious
- smoldered
- insurrection
- degraded
- status
- undercurrents
- sullen
- fluent
- gruff
- patriarch
- condescension
- regale
- fixated
- stifle
- uncharacteristically
- transformation
- mestizo
- design
- assessed

Chapter 9: Boy, *My brother's story*

Questions for review:
1. What kind of little boy is the girl's brother? How does he spend his days?
2. How does his life change when he becomes part of a group of older boys?
3. How is the boy different from his sister? What strengths does he have that she does not?

Personal reflection:
1. What was your childhood like? How did you spend your days? What did you do for fun?
2. How much freedom did you have as a child? Were your parents or caregivers strict or lenient?
3. Have you ever joined a peer group with its own rules and codes of conduct?

For further study:
1. Differences in how Latinos raise their children based on the child's gender; changes in modern times after the Women's Liberation Movement (1960s-1980s).
2. The importance of play in a child's development.
3. The dynamics of peer pressure for older children and adolescents.

Words to check out!
- brute
- sustained
- jaunts
- Caesar
- Shaolin monk
- cunning
- succumbed
- placid
- undertow
- shrouded
- tutelage
- randomly
- self-styled
- dreaded

- stoically
- imperiously
- ricocheting
- facet
- accomplice
- commence
- interlaced

Chapter 10: Fidencio Díaz, *Veteran, Teacher*

Questions for review:
1. What kind of bond does the girl's father have with Mr. Díaz?
2. Why does Mr. Díaz and his mother seem like they are from a "world apart?"
3. What kind of student was Mr. Díaz as a boy and as a teenager? How does he survive his unwelcoming environment?
4. What did Mr. Díaz do during the war? How did the war affect him?
5. What were Mr. Díaz' years at university like? What did he like to study?
6. What were Mr. Díaz' experiences as a teacher? Why is he compared to the "Spartan 300?"
7. When he visits churches, why does Mr. Díaz feel drawn to the photographs of soldiers who have died?

Personal reflection:
1. Can you describe one of your most notable and important teachers? What kind of person was she or he? How did they influence you?
2. Have you ever had a conflict with a teacher? Why? Was the conflict resolved?
3. Has someone you know served in the military? What was that experience like for them and the people in their lives?

For further study:
1. The histories of the estimated 1 million Hispanic/Latino soldiers who served in a succession of U.S. wars including World War I (1914-18), World War II (1939-1945), the Korean War (1950-1953), the Vietnam War (1962-1973), the Persian Gulf War (1990-91), and the wars in Iraq (2003-2011) and Afghanistan (2001-2021).
2. How the GI Bill (formally known as the Serviceman's Readjustment Act of 1944) provided educational and economic opportunity for millions of veterans.
3. Latino participation in higher education since WWII.
4. The challenges for Dreamers and other undocumented students; perspectives and policies across the U.S. political spectrum.
5. Thomas Jefferson (1743-1826), Jean-Jacques Rousseau (1712-

1778), and Ricardo Flores Magón (1873-1922). How their ideas helped shape the American (1775-1783), French (1789-1799), and Mexican (1910-1917) Revolutions.

Words to check out!
- predominated
- portly
- formal
- genial
- deferred
- scrawled
- intimidated
- even-tempered
- whimsical
- wrath
- dispassion
- muster
- compliance
- liberation
- threadbare
- moral
- sardonic
- compensation
- sardonic
- feints
- follies
- aura
- subterfuges
- potency
- subtle
- prevail
- furtively
- commandeered
- implacable
- foes
- equivalence
- depravity
- farce
- accounting
- full-fledged

- cadre
- monastic
- tragicomic
- shoddy
- pointed
- drawl
- the Ivies (Ivy League)
- sauntered
- pluck
- thrashed
- umpteenth
- self-reflection
- irony
- relished
- chachalacas
- buffoonery
- Spartan 300
- niche
- succession
- grove

Chapter 11: Foreign Queen, *My mother's story*

Questions for review:
1. How was the girl's mother's pueblo different from her father's pueblo?
2. How did the girl's mother prepare for marriage? What kind of high school student was she?
3. What was her mother's father like? What effect did he have on his family?
4. How did her mother access a college education?
5. Why did her parents marry?
6. What kind of mother did the girl have?
7. How did her mother adapt to marriage?
8. What was the one change of married life for which her mother was not prepared?
9. Why was the girl's mother a "foreign queen?"

Personal reflection:
1. What was your mother or other significant woman in your life like as a younger person? How did her family shape her views and prepare her for life?
2. Have you experienced substance use or observed it in the life of someone you know? How did it affect you or them? Did you or this person receive support?

For further study:
1. Effects of substance use in families.
2. College graduation rates for Latinas in the U.S.
3. Examples of the fates of "foreign queens" in world history.
4. The status of women in matriarchal societies.

Words to check out!
* matriarch
* chieftain
* throng
* cumulus
* extroverted
* tract
* idyllic
* unperturbed

- attributed
- counsel
- strictures
- steadfast
- stride
- cooed
- punctuated
- congenital
- flocked
- oasis
- avail
- gait
- slurred
- beseeching
- reoccurring
- sobriety

Chapter 12: Los Cedros, *My pueblo's story*

Questions for review:
1. What was the true history and reality of the U.S.-Mexico border of which the girl was unaware? Why was she unaware?
2. What did the girl think and feel about the Border Patrol? Why did she believe that her grandfather might get in trouble with them?
3. What were the mixed messages the girl received from her family and community about the Border Patrol and white people?
4. Why are the trees in Los Cedros described as "sentinels?"
5. What change happened in Los Cedros that finally weakened it decisively?
6. Why is the surveillance balloon described as a "Cyclops?"
7. Who does the writer suggest are responsible for the "era of the surveillance balloons and winged drones?"
8. How does she contrast the world of the social elites with the world of Los Cedros through the symbol of the pearl?
9. What does the woman feel her pueblo called her to do? How can she, as a writer, help her pueblo survive?

Personal reflection:
1. Describe your hometown. Why did you like or dislike that place? What was its history? What kind of neighbors or community did you have?
2. Have you ever had experience with U.S. Customs or Border Patrol? What was that experience like? Have you traveled to a foreign country and experienced their system for entry and border security?
3. What do you personally think about issues related to the U.S.-Mexico border including the Wall, the Family Separation Policy, vigilantes, or surveillance?

For further study:
1. History of the U.S.-Mexico border in Texas, California, Arizona, and New Mexico.
2. Changing views and policies on immigration; differences and similarities between the major political parties (Democrats and Republicans).
3. The Family Separation Policy.

4. Views on immigration in other countries across the globe.
5. The concept of the "imperishable" body in Buddhism, Christianity, and other world religions.

Words to check out!
- whitewashed
- lured
- craving
- rife
- illicit
- visors
- jesting
- pejoratives
- attributed
- state-sanctioned
- felled
- bleak
- succession
- drought
- sentinels
- akin
- maze
- amassing
- thunderous
- anesthetized
- advent
- surveillance
- Cyclops
- quivering
- coordinates
- drones
- condoned
- vigilance
- sentiments
- discreetly
- glimmer
- ogling
- vibrancy
- luster
- stately

- profound
- impervious
- infamy
- oblivion
- impenetrable

About the Author

Dorotea Reyna was born and raised in the Rio Grande Valley of South Texas, and earned a Bachelor's degree in English from Stanford University and a Master's degree in English from the University of Texas at Austin. Her poetry and fiction have appeared in several anthologies of Chicano literature including *New Chicana/Chicano Writing* (University of Arizona Press, 1992), *Entre Guadalupe y Malinche: Tejanas in Literature and Art* (University of Texas Press, 2016), and *Chicana/Latina Studies* (Journal of Mujeres Activas en Letras y Cambio Social, 2021).

Professionally, she began her career as an English Instructor at Texas A&I University (now Texas A&M University-Kingsville) and went on to serve as a fundraiser for the Hispanic Scholarship Fund and for several universities in the San Francisco Bay Area. A primary focus of her career has been on expanding access to higher education by raising scholarship funds for students with financial need, especially Latinos and other students of color.

www.ingramcontent.com/pod-product-compliance
Lightning Source LLC
Chambersburg PA
CBHW071213120626
46546CB00006B/2542